OPEN YOUR AKASHIC RECORDS

TRUST YOUR TRUTH, OPEN YOUR HEART TO
DEEP KNOWING, AND FIND YOUR SOUL'S
SPIRITUAL PRACTICE

CHERYL MARLENE

SOUL BRIGHT PRESS

Open Your Akashic Records:
Trust Your Truth,
Open Your Heart to Deep Knowing, and
Find Your Soul's Spiritual Practice

Published by
Soul Bright Press

Ebook ISBN: 978-1-945868-21-4

Audio ISBN: 978-1-945868-23-8

Print ISBN: 978-1-945868-22-1

LET'S CONNECT!

I'd love to connect with you!

To subscribe to my newsletter, work with me one-on-one, or jump into one of my wonderful Akashic Records learning programs, follow this link:

https://www.cherylmarlene.com/connect/

CONTENTS

INTRODUCTION

The Akashic Records snuck up on me. Initially I learned because I wanted to support a friend begin anew in her life as an Akashic Records teacher. I was not thinking about me and the possibilities of this new learning for myself.

My initial moments in the class foretold the essence of what is now more than twenty years of experience. I began with a huge release and a powerful mystical, visionary experience, solitary, the outlier in a large group.

Since then, I have been challenged to accept that I see the Akashic Records differently than most. My experience and understanding go far beyond the norm, into the edges of universal mystery and transcendent revelation. My willingness to accept this challenge has profoundly impacted the trajectory of my life, releasing years of trauma and disappointment. I have learned to trust myself, to accept my truth in each moment of my life. I have found me.

For You

In writing this book, my primary intention is to help you learn to trust yourself through the powerful process of self-discovery I offer within the Akashic Records. As you begin your own journey with the

Akashic Records, may you find within yourself your best self—through the focus of self-truth, self-discovery, and self-love. And like me, may you find your best life not in the destination but in your life's amazing journey.

Please allow the Akashic Records to help you see *you* so that you may learn to trust yourself. May your Akashic Records journey take you down your deep road of self-trust.

Self-First

Very intentionally, this book is for your own personal journey in the Akashic Records. Here you will learn to open only your Akashic Records. Learning to open the Akashic Records for another is a process for another time.

As you read and experience, you will find that learning for yourself first creates a firm foundation of trust in yourself and in the Akashic Records. Trust leads to truth. Yet, both truth and trust are necessary to have the confidence and compassion necessary to expand your Akashic Records journey beyond self.

This focus on self-first will also help you let go of anything within which might block clear connection with the Akashic Records on the deep road open to you. My intention is to help you move beyond platitudes and limitations into connection with the depth and power of your best self. As in any spiritual practice, you begin with self-first to connect with and experience the boundlessness of your amazing human experience.

Self-Discovery

Most methods for opening the Akashic Records focus on information. The opening method I share with you focuses on the Akashic Records as a spiritual process of self-discovery through the energy of your soul. This is why I think of the Akashic Records as the soul's spiritual practice.

The Akashic Records are not of the material world; they are of the infinite and eternal, the transcendent, the divine. As you will learn, the Akashic Records are not limited to the laws of linear human existence; they move beyond within the soul energy dynamics of the boundlessness and the mystical. The process you will learn and the experiences you will have form a vigorous spiritual practice which has the potential for both powerful and subtle personal transformation and integration. I will walk with you, offering support and guidance, so that you may step firmly into a new experience of your being and becoming.

Self-Truth

As we travel together into the Akashic Records, you will learn a new way of experiencing personal truth. In the process you will let go of whatever no longer serves the emerging new you. Along the way, you will also find yourself going deeper as you learn about yourself and your capacity to connect with your body, mind, heart, and soul through the perspective of your Akashic Records.

Self-Trust

When you are learning to open your Akashic Records, your greatest challenge will be trust. Trust has many important aspects including trust of yourself, trust of me and the process I offer, and trust in the Akashic Records as a source of truth and as a conduit of knowing, healing, and spiritual practice. The difference between a student who finds alignment and connection within her Akashic Records practice and a student who faces nothing but challenges is easy to explain. One has released blocks to trust and one has not.

The primary block to trusting yourself to open your Akashic Records … well … is you! The process of opening your Akashic Records is relatively easy. The difficult part is getting out of your own way.

Your path to trust is a firm foundation which clearly describes how and when and why you open your Akashic Records. This clarity helps you release blocks and whatever stands in your way. This isn't rocket science, but it may sometimes feel like you have launched yourself into the big, scary unknown. The entire experience of the content of this book is geared to helping you find your deepest layers of trust.

Self-Worth

Sometimes, mistakenly, perhaps you do not believe yourself worthy enough to open the Akashic Records. When self-confidence is not steady, perfection is erroneously deemed desirable in order to feel worthy of access to the Records.

Rest assured: perfection, in any form, is not required to open your Akashic Records. Rather, what is needed is a willingness to learn. Today, you are who you are and will learn what you learn. Tomorrow, you will begin with today's growth and build upon this foundation letting go of whatever does not serve in the moment. Learning is life's journey. You are always learning. The Akashic Records offer you a supportive, unlimited conduit to learning.

Most importantly, there is no end to achieve to be ready to open the Akashic Records. Begin today where you are. Know tomorrow you will shift and experience in a different way all which comes from learning to open your Akashic Records today.

Self-Study

For us both, this book is a journey. I come with you as a guide, as someone with prior experience to share with you, and as someone who understands both the excitement and the discomfort which accompanies personal spiritual growth.

You come as a beginner to this process of spiritual practice I offer in the Akashic Records. Because I know you are serious about the experience and learning of your spiritual path, the entire book is offered to you in support of you finding deep connection and awareness of yourself and your personal process of being and becoming.

Learning to open your Akashic Records is a progressive process which deepens with time and experience. Take each moment as it comes, let go of expectations, and enjoy your journey. At the end of the book I offer several options for follow-up and support.

You will soon see that you very quickly learn to open your Akashic Records, and most of the book is a series of practices aimed to help you establish trust in self, in the process, and with the Akashic Records. From this trust emerges the voice of your truth. Give yourself a chance to learn and experience the amazing depths within the Akashic Records and within you.

As you begin to read, two options are available to you. One is to read the book, start to finish, skipping around, or in any way you feel drawn. Choosing this option is reading from an informational perspective.

The second option is to use this book as a guided experience, allowing you the opportunity to learn, coupled with the potential of greatly enhancing and changing your life. Understand that this is not "just a read." With this in mind, I have intentionally arranged the material to move you sequentially through multiple layers of depth, even reminding you to step away. Read a bit, and then take a break, allowing what you have ingested to settle and move you. I hope you choose the second option. Though, as in all things, the choice is yours.

Welcome!

I offer you this book as firm foundation to support your journey in the Akashic Records. May your journey be life-changing, joyful, and deeply moving as new levels of self-trust open your heart. Life is truly amazing!

In Joy!

Cheryl

PS. A Reader's Packet which contains PDFs and an audio recording to support your learning process is also available Download here: https://www.cherylmarlene.com/yourown/

SECTION I

YOUR JOURNEY

The journey of a thousand miles
Begins with one step
Made, here, now.
Beyond destination,
Journey is your experience of life
Lived fully in this moment,
Opening always
to who you become in your next step.
Soul illuminating, heart opening, you begin.

1

BEGINNING YOUR JOURNEY

A journey is a motion through time and space. Adding a spiritual dimension, journey is motion through the spiritual and physical aspects of your body, mind, heart, and soul.

When I first began my journey in the Akashic Records, I thought I was headed somewhere, a destination, a predefined place for myself. Instead, I found that the spiritual practice of the Akashic Records, in its most important perspective, is not a defined point of arrival like an answer or provable truth. Instead, the journey of the Akashic Records moves within the essential core of who you are and can become. The essence of you is eternal and infinite. However, your experience of you shifts from moment to moment as you learn and expand, presenting what can feel like a moving target.

As you begin, the challenge is to understand the destination is never attained because that's not the point of the journey. The purpose of the journey is to learn about the amazing motion of your true, eternal essence. In my experience, learning to open your Akashic records is fundamentally a lesson in trust and truth. You begin a never-ending journey into the depths of you, and who you are in this moment, and the amazing potential you have to become, based on the following concepts.

**Self-trust is your path to hearing your truth.
Hearing and recognizing your truth reinforces your ability to trust.**

Trust leads to truth leads to trust: in a continual spiral path of opening, discovery, and integration.

Learning to open your Akashic Records is a spiritual practice which helps you develop trust in yourself.

As self-trust deepens, your ability to hear and understand the truth of who you are, and can become, expands.

Envision a lotus blossom, rising in trust from the pond's muck to reveal the luminous essence of truth.

Learning to open your Akashic Records is lotus-like: a beautiful, revelatory process of self-illumination.

Learning the process of opening your Akashic Records can be done in sixty minutes.

Learning to *trust* yourself within your connection with your Akashic Records is an unfolding, progressive process of self-discovery lasting a lifetime.

. . .

Begin where you are now, ready to learn and journey, allowing the illumination of you to light your path.

Let us begin . . . .

2

YOUR DOOR OPENS

L*ife always seems to move beyond expectation—thankfully!*

Learning to trust my journey within the Akashic Records has always moved me beyond expectation. The beginning of my journey was no exception; with only two years of experience, my Guides began asking me to teach. I resisted with all my might because I didn't feel ready. But, after several months of persistent assurance, I was ready, I realized that the deeper resistance on my part was fear: raw, stark, gut-clenching, existing within me between two opposites. On one hand was failure and the sense of not being good enough, and on the other side was apprehension about stepping into my greatness. I felt caught, floating away from the shore of stability where I thought I knew my life, but not yet ready to accept that I had the power to be more in a different way.

In response to my request to tell me how the Akashic Records work, my Guides offered up an elegant response, clear in its simplicity yet deep with complexity. I will go into this in detail later. For now, let me summarize what I received as the soul energy dynamics of the Akashic Records.

Instead of a library metaphor, my Guides explained the Akashic Records as energetic ebb and flow from the divine boundlessness to the beauty of physical manifestation. An eternal return of energy from spiritual to physical to spiritual —an unending, interactive dynamic.

Receiving this perspective coincided with my new experience within my Akashic Records which I identify as research. Over the next year, I increased my research, prepared to teach, and dove into understanding the soul energy dynamics of the Akashic Records. I also learned a soul.dance between the poles of my fear and found a higher ground which integrated these opposites. This personal motion supported me to explore and understand the Akashic Records at progressively deeper levels.

Knowing. Healing. Spiritual practice. Much is possible and theoretically there are no limits within the Akashic Records. Yet all activity in the Records, at its essential level, is one or more of these three primary expressions. Understanding this idea then rocked my world and sent me on a path of teaching because it became my journey of trust, truth, and the release of fear.

The soul energy dynamics of the Akashic Records emerge with the idea that the fundamental nature of the Akashic Records is energetic. To understand the Akashic Records as energy, the beginning is always:

Everything is energy.
All energy exists on a continuum from potential to form.

Potential   Form

At the potential end of the continuum, the Akashic Records are about knowing, the process of how you know. Potential arises from divine source as infinite and eternal expression to flow into physical form.

On the form end of the continuum, the Akashic Records are about information because this is the form knowing takes as it moves from spiritual to physical.

The Akashic Records exist across the entirety of the energy continuum. This means that the Akashic Records are not just a source of information. The Akashic Records are a process which emerges from divine knowing and supports you in discovering your own process of knowing.

This is an important distinction as you begin. You open your Akashic Records not just for answers but to develop and refine your own process of trusting yourself to receive your truth. Opening your Akashic Records is not a matter of right or wrong. As spiritual practice, opening is about balance and alignment, connection and resonance. Learning trust within the Akashic Records helps you learn to trust yourself to receive your truth in all aspects of your life.

Because the Akashic Records exist across the entirety of the energy continuum, the Records are accessible in various ways within the different aspects of the continuum from potential to form.

The method you will learn here accesses the Akashic Records within potential, from within the energy of the origin of your soul. With this intention, you will learn to step into the perspective of your soul and see not just from the body's point of view but from the perspective of your soul.

Accessing in this way creates the opportunity for you to begin a journey within the deep road of the Akashic Records. This deep road is both metaphor for, and direct experience of, the deep unknown as it melts into the infinite unknowable. Not to worry—you will begin within the energy which resonates with you. With practice, and as your trust expands, the deep road will open naturally for you, allowing your exploration into the depth you desire and yearn to experience.

————

There are two avenues to your Akashic Records. One is to ask someone who knows how to open yours for you. The other avenue is to learn to open them for yourself.

Opening the Akashic Records for yourself opens the door of possibility to powerful experiences which include these three essential experiences:

- Knowing
- Healing
- Spiritual Practice

The Akashic Records as Knowing

The most profound aspect of the Akashic Records is its connection to divine knowing.

Knowing is the process of being aware of what and how you know. Knowing is gathering through your awareness that which you can know from your consciousness and unconsciousness, and from the known and the unknown.

When you learn to open your own Records, you are learning to connect through your soul's origin to divine knowing. Learning to do this heightens your ability to feel and receive, within yourself, when you are in your Akashic Records.

Additionally, this is a skill transferable outside of your Records within your everyday life. Learning to be subtly aware of knowing within the Records helps you learn to follow this same level of subtle awareness within the day-to-day activities of your life.

Learning how to connect with the knowing of the Akashic Records is a process of trust and a process of learning to hear your truth. By becoming comfortable with truth and trust within your own Records, you create the possibility of being able to hear and to receive truth and act within trust outside of the Akashic Records.

Know that the Akashic Records have no intent to create dependency. There is no expectation that you should come to your Akashic Records for answers to every question and decision in your life. Quite the contrary, the intent is independence and the focus is on truth and trust. You are an amazing human being and have the capacity for greatness every day. The Akashic Records want nothing more than to foster this independence that you may claim the deep truth of your deepest expression as a fully integrated spiritual-physical being.

The Akashic Records as Healing

The Akashic Records are always in balance, always aware where balance is, and respond to you within an awareness of your balance. Therefore, balance is not something that needs to be created. Balance always is.

Healing is balance. The energetic shift called healing is experienced when balance is felt. Thus, in the Akashic Records, at its most primary level, healing is awareness of where balance is in the present moment. Learning how to focus on knowing as a process supports your ability to feel balance because the feeling of balance comes through the same process of awareness as does knowing.

Additionally, in their deepest resonant state, the Akashic Records exist within the 100% potential energy of the infinite and the eternal. When you enter the Akashic Records at the deepest level, you enter this level of resonance, and a field of energy is created between your energy and the potential energy of the Akashic Records.

The nature of all energy fields is to come into equilibrium. For example, mixing hot water with cold water yields warm water. However, the pure potential of the infinite and eternal will always maintain itself as 100% potential energy. Thus, to come into equilibrium, when entering the Akashic Records, the effect of the joined energy fields will raise the resonance of your energy field into equilibrium with the pure potential of the Akashic Records.

Experiencing this level of resonance and feeling balance in this heightened energy state will support a healing shift towards greater balance within the circumstances of life. This is energetic healing on all levels, body, mind, heart, and soul.

This fundamental nature of healing in the Akashic Records has incredible potential and is just beginning to be investigated. Openness to learning is the entry point, moving beyond stereotype, it provides unexpected depth and unexpected, joyful, powerful experience.

The Akashic Records as Spiritual Practice

The experience of accessing knowing and healing within the Akashic Records is a conscious process which has a defined set of steps to follow and a set of agreements which provide an ethical framework. As you open your Akashic Records and have the experience of the subtle knowing and healing shift, your life begins to find more clarity, you begin to feel more at ease and in balance with yourself, and you find you are able to trust the truth of yourself.

Integral to your spiritual journey is the inner work you do with yourself to understand where you are, who you are, and what you can become. Spiritual practice is the tool of this inner work. Spiritual practice can be a formal exercise, though it need not be because the essence of spiritual practice lies within conscious intention.

The whole point of spiritual practice is to learn something new about yourself rather than reinforcing outdated beliefs. If you take the defensive, knee-jerk approach of I KNOW, then you will miss the opportunity inherent in I LEARN.

The process of learning to open your Akashic Records and then the practice of opening your Akashic Records on a consistent basis is spiritual practice in its most essential expression.

Within the experience of opening your Akashic Records, knowing and healing join with spiritual practice as the three most important reasons for you to learn to open your Akashic Records. In doing so, you are learning to connect with the deepest, most amazing parts of yourself and stepping into a place of continual self-discovery and personal spiritual development.

———

To open your Akashic Records, you will bring together these four elements:

- **Agreements**: a set of statements which guide and define when and how you open the Akashic Records.
- **Visualization**: a simple set of instructions which visually guide you to the entrance of your Akashic Records.
- **Blessing**: words of intention for your entry and experience in your Akashic Records.

- **Process**: based on your agreements, the method you use, putting the visualization and blessing together to open your Akashic Records.

In the next chapters, I share exactly how to bring these components together with step-by-step instructions for your first experience of opening your Akashic Records.

Take a deep breath!

3

AGREEMENTS

*An agreement is a clear statement of intention
between two or more people.*

To open your Akashic Records, you are asked to make agreements with the Akashic Records and with me which guide how and when you open the Akashic Records. These agreements support your process of opening and the use of the blessing you will learn in the next lesson.

These agreements are sacred and ask you to step forward in your experience with the Akashic Records with integrity and in truth. Forming the ethical framework of your Akashic Records practice, these agreements have important implications for you as you step into this new aspect of your life.

Accessing the Akashic Records is not done on a whim or to entertain. Entering into the Akashic Records is a serious spiritual endeavor. The

Agreements support and assure sacred space for you when you enter and ask with integrity, clear intention, and an open mind and heart.

Serious in intent and broad in scope, your firm foundation begins by understanding and accepting these agreements.

Each time you open your Akashic Records, you are embarking on a journey. Therefore, the Agreements are based on the five steps of the spiritual journey. To facilitate understanding, I present the Agreements one by one and discuss the importance of each component, so you are clear and can freely make these Agreements.

---

1. I am Beginner's Mind

The first step of the spiritual journey is The Call. The Call is awareness that there is something for you to do or experience. When you learn to open your Akashic Records, you are answering a call. You may not know why you are being called. Yet, at some point in the future you will understand the why.

Within The Call, the primary spiritual concept is beginner's mind. In beginner's mind you are open to learn. Instead of saying, "Oh! I know that!" You are saying, "I am here to learn!" This attitude of learning is as true on the first day you enter into your Akashic Records as it is twenty years later. You're always a beginner, always approaching the Akashic Records as a learner.

To enter the Akashic Records with beginner's mind, you make these agreements:

I begin each opening of the Akashic Records being as clear and open as I can.

Open your Records when you are feeling clear and healthy. If you have a cold or do not feel well, this isn't the best time. However, if you feel down or out of sorts, don't hold back because being in the Records can help shift your attitude.

I move inward to answer The Call, letting go of ego.

I define ego as the inflexibility of self. To answer The Call, one needs to be able to step away from expectations and rigid beliefs to hear something new. The same flexibility is needed within the Akashic Records, otherwise you will only receive the contents of your own mind.

I am in training for twelve months from this day, _____ (enter date).

To reinforce the idea of you as beginner, you agree to be in training for a year. Though remember, within the Records, you will always be learning.

I will begin each time like the first time. I will not memorize the Blessing. I will say the blessing out loud.

By not memorizing the blessing, you must bring yourself into your awareness and think about what you are doing each time you open your Records. This helps reinforce your approach as a beginner. I keep my blessing written on an index card kept in my

Akashic Records journal plus copies in my purse and on my phone.

Each time you open your Akashic Records, you will say the blessing out loud, with enough volume to hear the words. A whisper is acceptable providing you can hear what you say.

---

2. I am here, now in the Present Moment.

The second step on your spiritual journey is preparation, doing what you need to do to be able to answer The Call. Whatever you have done to get to this moment of learning to open your Akashic Records is preparation. This process of preparation is also one of inner clearing and of inner awareness, letting go of old stories, limiting beliefs, and all that is not essentially you to create space within.

Within preparation, the primary spiritual concept is present moment. Be here, now. The Akashic Records flow from the present moment. Thus, your awareness needs to be in this moment, now, in order to connect and receive from the Akashic Records. Fear and blame, in particular, divert attention from the present. Blame is a pull to the past and fear is a push into the future. Complete elimination is not required to enter the Akashic Records. Instead, learn to be aware when either appears and blocks your path. Put them to the side where they can be dealt with either while in the Records or after closing.

To enter the Akashic Records within the present moment, you make these agreements:

I gather my energy and awareness into this Present Moment.

You begin by bringing your awareness into this moment, letting go of anything which keeps you from being fully present.

I let my expectations, presumptions and judgments go. I let go of blame and fear. I let go of stories that no longer serve me.

In other words, you are letting go of whatever doesn't serve as you enter your Akashic Records. To open, you don't need to solve anything or be in a better, clearer space. You are not asked to come to the Akashic Records as a perfect human being. What you don't want is to bring in stuff which may get in your way. Often that which you identify as standing in your way is something you may want to ask about in your Records. I think of putting my concerns on the back burner, or to the side and slightly behind me, where they are not energetically standing in front of me and causing interference. Don't build a wall. Instead, put your concerns in a basket and retrieve each item when you are in your Akashic Records asking for understanding, or attend to the basket after you close.

Imagine you are at the beach watching the waves roll in. The ocean and the waves flow on their own. You don't make the flow happen. Building a wall in front of the ocean does not stop the flow. However, your doubts, uncertainties, and concerns will act like a wall if you bring them along as you open your Records.

If drugs, alcohol, or other stimulants are a problem for me, I will not consume those 12 hours prior to opening my Akashic Records.

Please notice I say "if." Also note that I am not just referring to drugs or alcohol. These may be the most common interferences, but not the only ones. The point is to pay attention to yourself and what causes interference for you. Possibilities also include sugar, caffeine, or a lack of sleep. If there is something you identify, then give yourself a break to allow your brain to clear and your body to relax. For example, I do not drink alcohol the night before I work with clients in their Akashic Records. I do this not because I have a problem with alcohol. Instead, I do this to honor and respect the people I work with. Pay attention to yourself. Show yourself honor and respect.

3. I set my Intention without external influence

On your spiritual journey, the third step is initiation, a learning of the knowledge and skills needed to be able to answer The Call. New knowledge, new practice, new points of view, new ways of being are all essential. Experiencing this book is initiation for your Akashic Records. Even at this stage, you may not understand the entirety of your call to journey, but through truth, faith, and intention, initiation brings your attention to what you will need to complete your journey.

For initiation, the primary spiritual concept is intention. Everything comes from the Records through stating intention and is usually done by asking questions. I often phrase intention in the Akashic Records as, "What do you want to know?" When you open your Akashic Records, you come with your intention, what you want to know. Others may suggest questions for you to ask, but you must have desire to understand for anything you bring to your Akashic Records.

Whatever your intention, you do not need to worry about stating it perfectly. The blessing you will use clarifies intention as "deepest intent for highest path." Don't worry about stating the question perfectly. That's unnecessary blame and judgment on self. Trust that you ask the question which needs to be asked in the moment. Trust that the full extent of your intention will be expressed both consciously and unconsciously. The Akashic Records respond to the fullness of you and not just to the specific words you use.

To enter the Akashic Records with intention, you make these agreements:

I identify what I want to ask the Akashic Records.

What do you want to know? What do you want to let go? Begin with these ideas and let your questions and intention develop from within. I don't write down my questions, but across the top of my journal page I do write down one or two words as a reminder for each question I want to ask as I work in my Records.

I focus my entire self on receiving everything that is for me, in this present moment, from the Akashic Records.

Bringing your entire self into the moment helps you connect more deeply and with keener awareness of the flow of your Records. Notice when you can't be present and feel into what this might be about.

I listen with my heart.

In your Akashic Records, you will want to listen with your heart so that you can catch the subtleties and the nuances which your mind may miss. The mind can get caught up with rational analysis whereas your heart will open to receive the gentle whispers offered by your Records in response to your intention. I always write down everything I receive when I open my Records. The act of writing occupies my mind so that my heart is free to receive and process.

I open the Akashic Records for myself only. I will not open the Akashic Records for another person or entity.

Very simply: you are engaged now in a process of learning for yourself. You are learning about responsibility for yourself and not for another. This is a matter of integrity with yourself, with the Akashic Records, and with me. Opening for another may come, but not now.

4. I maintain Integrity with myself and others.

The fourth step of the spiritual journey is transformation. If you have been traveling up a mountain on your journey, transformation is getting to the peak and experiencing an "Aha!" moment. In this moment, you experience a shift and see clearly what in the moment before was murky at best. Transformation occurs in the moment when you release your limiting stories, judgments, and fears. When you willingly allow yourself to stand in that vulnerable place of observation of all your warts and disfigurements, hopes and dreams.

Transformation begins in the moment you risk all to come face to face with the powerful truth of your deepest being.

In transformation, the primary spiritual concept is integrity. Do you trust yourself and can others trust you to do what you say you will do? More than honesty, integrity is taking the responsibility to attend to the consequences of your words and actions especially when what you intended did not transpire. Within the Akashic Records integrity shows first in whether you keep these Agreements and, thereafter, with all actions, words, and commitments both within and outside of the Akashic Records. Remember working in the Akashic Records will have profound effects on all aspects of your life. As you maintain integrity, your alignment with integrity will expand.

To enter the Akashic Records with integrity, you make these agreements:

I agree to always be honest and seek balance and understanding with the Akashic Records.

As you experience the Akashic Records, your sense of honesty, your openness to understanding, and your awareness of balance will deepen and expand. Clarity will develop and your capacity for integrity will blossom.

I acknowledge Cheryl Marlene as my Akashic Records Teacher and will turn to her as needed for assistance and knowing.

The nature of the Akashic Records is a collective awareness referred to as the Master, Teachers, and Loved Ones. By learning to open the Akashic Records through my book and through me, you are accepting and acknowledging that I, Cheryl Marlene, am your legacy connection with the Akashic Records. All that I offer is aimed at helping you develop a firm foundation to open your Akashic Records and support a lifelong learning process through the Akashic Records.

I keep the process of opening the Akashic Records to myself and will honor others as they find their own path in the Akashic Records.

Holding sacred your process and connection to the Akashic Records supports you in many deep and powerful ways. Respecting yourself and the Akashic Records opens doors to deeper parts of the Akashic Records. In learning to open the Akashic Records, you are learning for yourself. Integrity is reinforced by allowing others to come to this spiritual practice in their own way.

I will not teach another person how to open the Akashic Records.

This is not a book which teaches you how to teach. This is a book which helps you learn for yourself. You are a beginner in the Akashic Records. Honor yourself and respect the Akashic Records by refraining from teaching another at this point.

---

5. I am Sacred Space.

The spiritual journey finishes its motion in integration. Integration is coming down from the mountain top and making the journey's learning part of your everyday life. Many are enticed to stay on the mountain top within the secure feeling of transformation, journey uncompleted. Integration asks you to bring together heart and mind, physical and spiritual, within and without into your everyday life. Moving beyond the mountain top, integration asks that you step forward with all of who you are, imperfections and dreams, warts, scars, and hard-won understandings of life's truths. Integration is the opportunity to join all your parts together in whatever manner may serve your truth in this moment and to move forward as an integrated person. Yet integration will not happen if you hold yourself apart.

The primary concept of integration is sacred space. To create sacred space in the Akashic Records, there are four necessary elements: beginner's mind, present moment, intention, and integrity. All that you have agreed to up to this point becomes integral in your ability to hold sacred space for yourself and your journey within your Akashic Records.

To create sacred space in the Akashic Records, you make these agreements:

My clear intention and integrity form the foundation for my connection with the Akashic Records. I yield control and step into faith with trust.

The firm foundation of your Akashic Records connection is established with your clear intention and your willingness to maintain integrity. What happens in your experience is not under your control any more than you can control the ebb and flow of the ocean. Each time you open your Akashic Records is an act of faith which requires your trust. Trust is the foundation of your path. Trust emerges within you through your experience and as you release blocks which do not serve your journey in your Akashic Records.

I will not change my blessing or process for opening the Akashic Records nor use another method of accessing the Akashic Records during my twelve-month training period.

You are a beginner and here to learn. Do not presume you know. The elements of the process and blessing are intentional and arranged to support your firm foundation with the Akashic Records. Don't mix and match. Give yourself time to step into the depth and fullness supported by the process offered in this book. Only with experience and practice will the deeper road reveal itself and only if you are able to maintain a firm foundation. All the process elements I offer are geared to help you. Resist your urge to fiddle at least until your training period is complete.

I will open the Akashic Records only when I need them and only in a space of safety and full concentration.

When you open your Akashic Records, do so in a quiet location where you will not be interrupted. Do what feels good and right to you: burn sage or incense, hold a crystal or other gemstone, use pen and paper. Create a ritual for yourself. Yet, do not become rigid within the ritual. Do not set yourself up in such a way that the surroundings must be perfect to feel you can connect with your Akashic Records. On one side, ritual is supportive. But on the other, over-reliance on ritual may inhibit.

The goal is to feel so powerfully connected and able in your Akashic Records that you can open your Records in the worst possible location or situation—like a crowded sports stadium or a shopping mall. Not that you would open the Records in either location, but you could if necessary. I often open my Records outside, along a mountain trail, or sitting on the beach. I do not require anything other than pen, paper, and a copy of my blessing.

Making Agreements

Here are the Agreements. Read them! Ask yourself if you can agree. And when you know you can, sign and date. (The Reader's Packet has a PDF of the Agreements for you to print: https://www.cherylmarlene.com/yourown/)

Agreements:
Open Your Akashic Records

1. I am Beginner's Mind.

1. I begin each opening of the Akashic Records being as clear and open as I can.
2. I move inward to answer The Call, letting go of ego.
3. I am in training for twelve months from this day, _____(enter date).
4. I will begin each time like the first time.

5. I will not memorize the Blessing. I will say the blessing out loud.

2. I am here, now in the Present Moment.

1. I gather my energy and awareness into this Present Moment.
2. I let go of my expectations, presumptions and judgments.
3. I let go of blame and fear.
4. I let go of my stories that no longer serve me.
5. If drugs, alcohol, or other stimulants are a problem for me, I will not consume those 12 hours prior to opening my Akashic Records.

3. I set my Intention without external influence.

1. I identify what I want to ask the Akashic Records.
2. I focus my entire self on receiving everything that is for me, in this moment, from the Akashic Records.
3. I listen with my heart.
4. I open the Akashic Records for myself only. I will not open the Akashic Records for another person or entity.

4. I maintain Integrity with myself and others.

1. I agree to always be honest and seek balance and understanding within the Akashic Records.
2. I acknowledge Cheryl Marlene as my Akashic Records Teacher and will turn to her as needed for assistance and knowing.
3. I keep the process of opening the Akashic Records to myself and will honor others as they find their own path in the Akashic Records.
4. I will not teach another person how to open the Akashic Records.

5. I am Sacred Space.

1. My clear intention and integrity form the foundation for my connection with the Akashic Records. I yield control and step into faith with trust.
2. I will not change my blessing or process for opening the Akashic Records nor use another method of accessing the Akashic Records during my twelve-month training period.
3. I will open the Akashic Records only when I need them and only in a space of safety and full concentration.

Signed:

Date:

4

VISUALIZATION

W hen I first learned to open the Akashic Records, I did not learn with a visualization, just a blessing. Though I was able to connect, I felt mis-connected like there was static in the channel. I also felt ungrounded in a way that might not be healthy for me over the long run. I asked my Records for assistance and received what I present to you now.

Since incorporating this visualization into my process and with a few of adjustments over the years, I now feel an extremely clear connection. In the beginning, I felt jerked out of my body on opening. Now I feel a simple turn of my head and I'm connected. Though experience affects opening, refining and expanding connection, the visualization has made a huge difference. As I will explain, the Akashic Records surprised me in both simplicity and complexity, offering a visualization which creates focus, reinforces concentration, and offers a path for aligned, resonating absorption. The visualization also offers grounding, balancing, and centering energetically in a much more complex and healthy way than is typical for these techniques.

Over the years, I've had students both love and resist the visualization. Resistance comes in part from those who do not "see" a visualization. If you are like this, do not worry. Let your resistance release. Seeing is not required.

Instead, feel. Feel yourself moving through what is suggested. Feel the path, feel the balance, feel the motion of your connection.

Other students resist the control of exactly what, when, and where. If you feel yourself chafing a bit, lean yourself into the imaginative possibilities of the visualization to feel that the process is your choice and one of support rather than a forced direction.

Also note your experience in this step and in all steps which follow. While you may be here to learn to work with the Akashic Records, this is not the only learning. Additionally, learning comes within your whole, full picture and may sneak up on you when least expected. If you feel resistance, what about your experience is bringing this up in this moment? If you feel anger, why?

A visualization is a set of steps you see or feel, taking you on a journey. Each step asks you to do, create, see, or feel something as you progress.

The first steps of the visualization create safe space for your journey. The next steps lead you from this physical world to the spiritual energy of divine knowing and the origin of your soul where your Akashic Records are located.

This visualization does something a bit unusual. Instead of specifically grounding or centering, you are creating balance for yourself between heaven and earth. It is very important to find this balance as you enter your Akashic Records. You do not need to worry about either grounding or centering first because the process of the visualization does this for you, plus much more.

Additionally, there is very clear intention not to use chakras, meridians, or other physical energy centers for connection. Please avoid shifting the process to do this. You will miss the deeper spiritual connection if you insist on intentionally including these pathways.

Also, please note that the visualization has important elements which must remain part of your visualizing process. However, the nature of the elements may change over time. For example, a tree must always be part of the beginning. Yet today the tree might be a maple tree and tomorrow a pine tree.

If you do not retrieve the Reader's Pack (https://www.cherylmarlene. com/yourown/) from my website which includes an audio recording of the visualization, then I recommend that you read and record the visualization for your initial use. Over time, you will learn and become confident that you can follow the visualization without audio cues. In the beginning, hearing the visualization is most helpful and reduces the number of elements which need to be remembered as you open your Akashic Records.

These are the key elements of the visualization which must always be part of your opening process:

1. Find a tree and a safe, comfortable place.
2. Breath in the energy of the earth through the soles of your feet.
3. Bring in the energy of the heavens through the top of your head.
4. Feel the center of your body wherever you feel this to be. It isn't necessarily one specific point or another because each person feels this differently.
5. Feel balanced between heaven and earth.
6. Follow a path from center.
7. Find an entryway at the end of the path.

In the next lesson, you will learn to use the visualization within the process of opening your Akashic Records. Please read through this right now. Now is also the time to make the recording of the visualization if that is your choice.

Visualization:
Balance Between Heaven and Earth

Take a deep breath and release. Take another deep breath and release.

Begin by thinking of a tree and a safe, comfortable place. The tree can be real; the tree can be invented. The place can be real or invented. Put your tree in your safe, comfortable place, adjusting either the tree or the place so that they go together and you feel safe and comfortable about both.

In your mind's eye, walk up to the tree. Feel its form; feel its beauty. Turn and stand with your back against the tree, your spine aligned with the trunk of the tree, your feet in amongst the roots and the earth at the base of the trunk, your head towards the top of the tree.

Now, feel your feet melt into the earth and the roots of the tree, and as you breathe in, feel the energy of the earth come up through the soles of your feet, up your legs and into the center of your body wherever you feel your center to be.

As you breathe in, bring the energy of the earth up through the soles of your feet, and into the center of your body.

Now, turn your attention to the top of your head, the top of the tree, and to the sky and stars and heavens above.

As you breathe out, bring the energy of the heavens down through the top of the tree, the top of your head, down into the center of your body wherever you feel the center to be. As you breathe out, bring down the energy of the heavens through the top of your head and into the center of your body.

As you breathe in, bring in the energy of the earth and as you breathe out, bring in the energy of the heavens. As you breathe in and breathe out, feel heaven and earth meet at the center of your body.

As you breathe in and breathe out, feel yourself perfectly balanced between heaven and earth.

As you continue to breathe in and breathe out, focus at the center of your body where heaven and earth meet. See or feel a path extend from your center.

Follow this path wherever it leads you until you get to the end of the path. You will know the end because there will be some type of entryway: a door, a curtain, or a gate.

When you arrive at the entryway, open your eyes, say your blessing out loud, and open your Akashic Records.

5

BLESSING

E very time I say the blessing, I feel the brush of connection with that which is beyond me. I feel me aligning with the balance of the Akashic Records. At first, I didn't feel this at all. Instead I felt a tug and a jerk. Yet, with practice, my experience shifted. I shifted, and my expectations dissolved.

I have seen students with the same struggle give up too quickly as well as persevere despite the initial challenge. Other students have settled in immediately only to feel thwarted several months later. There is no "right" way to learn and to enter. There is only your path, your experience, your understanding.

In awe, the words of the blessing are universal connection, creative, uplifting, directive, and supportive. The blessing offers a focus, a point of concentration, a way to combat the over-rationality of the mind. The blessing is your heart giving voice to the purpose of its path and the possibilities of full awareness of the amazing motion of the Akashic Records. Words of power, of gratitude, and of connection to illuminate the journey of your soul. Namaste.

. . .

Your Akashic Records blessing is an invocation of support for you as you embark on your journey within your Akashic Records. The blessing has two parts. The opening section is used within the opening process each time you open your Akashic Records. The closing section is part of the process for closing your Records.

Remembering your Agreements, there are two very important ideas to understand about your blessing:

You do not memorize the blessing.

Each opening of the Akashic Records is done within beginner's mind. To do this you do not memorize the blessing. Of course, over time and with frequent use, you may very well remember the words. However, you put no intention into memorization. Instead, write the blessing on an index card, print it on a piece of paper, or put it in a safe place on your phone. Each time you open your Akashic Records, bring out your blessing and recite it at the appropriate moment within the opening process. This relieves you of the pressure of remembering and frees your attention to concentrate on the opening process.

You always say the blessing out loud.

You do not need to yell, but when you say the blessing, your voice needs to be audible. A soft whisper works. You must be able to hear what you say. Why? Saying the blessing out loud creates an anchor between where you are in this moment and with the non-physical energy of your Akashic Record. I cannot over-stress the importance of saying the blessing out loud.

Also, remember in your Agreements, you agreed to not change your Blessing.

———

Let's review the Blessing!

Opening:

Be with me in spirit as I cross the threshold of divine love and light.

This acknowledges that, as you open your Akashic Records, you are crossing from this physical world into divine knowing and the origin of your soul. Opening your Akashic Records is a liminal experience. It takes you across a threshold between the physical and the spiritual, between here and now, into the infinite and the eternal.

Hold me in your loving embrace as I open my heart and mind to the Masters, Teachers and Loved Ones of my soul's Akashic Record.

Asking for support, you are opening both your heart and mind and focusing on the collective wisdom of divine assistance which surrounds and imbues your Akashic Record.

Support me as I let my troubles slide away.

Here you declare your intention to release, in this moment, anything which might stand in your way as you open your Akashic Records. Remember, this isn't about solving everything before opening. This is about not bringing barriers to entry along in the opening process.

In response to my deepest intent show me my highest path.

No matter your intention, this statement declares the broadest parameter of your intention. Deepest and highest is a phrase for the entirety of you spiritually and physically. Thus, anything you ask within your Akashic Records will be framed within the metaphors of your deepest and your highest across body, mind, heart, and soul.

When we are done, release me in love and joy, keeping my energy raised.

Now you declare how you would like to complete your journey. You are asking that any shifts which you experience, within the 100% potential energy of the Akashic Records, return with you and be accessible to you after you have closed your Records.

I, (state full legal name), stand ready for whatever is for me, Now.

Your full legal name is what is on your driver's license or passport. This is not a nickname, or a name given to you by a revered teacher. This is also not a maiden name or birth name that has since been legally changed. Your full legal name as it is right now.

In this statement you are also declaring the present moment as your focus. Now. Not yesterday, not tomorrow. Now.

The Records are open.

> In the process, you will learn exactly when to say this last statement of the opening.

Closing:

In love and light, I thank my Masters, Teachers, and Loved Ones for their information and guidance.

> Expressing gratitude is an essential part of this blessing and is the first statement every time you close your Records.

Amen. Amen. Amen.

> The first Amen brings you out of your Akashic Records. The second brings you past the threshold between spiritual and physical, and the third brings you back into your physical space.

The Records are closed.

> Again, said out loud, this last statement closes your Akashic Records.

Blessing:
Open Your Akashic Records

Opening:

Be with me in spirit as I cross the threshold of divine love and light. Hold me in your loving embrace as I open my heart and mind to the Masters, Teachers and Loved Ones of my soul's Akashic Record. Support me as I let my troubles slide away. In response to my deepest intent, show me my highest path. When we are done, release me in love and joy, keeping my energy raised. I, (state full legal name), stand ready for whatever is for me Now.

The Records are open.

Closing:

In love and light, I thank my Masters, Teachers, and Loved Ones for their information and guidance. Amen. Amen. Amen.

The Records are closed.

6

PROCESS

Now the elements come together. The process describes how to use the visualization and blessing to open your Akashic Records. As you begin to open your Akashic Records, I have several guidelines for you to follow:

Use your common sense.

Whatever the Akashic Records might suggest to you, filter everything through your common sense, through what you know to be true about you. Often what is suggested is meant metaphorically rather than literally. If a suggestion is made that you don't want to follow, don't do it! Your Akashic Records want to support you and they don't want to make things difficult. If you don't understand, ask for clarification. If you don't like a suggestion, ask for an alternative.

BREATHE!

When you get nervous, there is a tendency to hold your breath. Yet, in the Akashic Records, breath is what keeps the flow moving. I cannot over-stress the importance of breathing. While it's not necessary to use a special type of breath, you do need to be allowing yourself to inhale and exhale in a steady, regular rhythm. If something seems to be not flowing, not working, not something: BREATHE! Breath initiates and continues the energy flow of your Akashic Records.

Keep eyes open.

Except in the opening process where eyes closed is most effective, when you are in the Akashic Records keep your eyes open. At times, you might use a soft focus or lightly close your eyes to see or receive, but that's occasional not all the time. When you are in your Akashic Records, you will be writing down what you receive, and this will help you keep your eyes open.

Healthy and well for clarity and deeper connection.

If you are sick or feeling energetically depleted, this is not a good time to open your Akashic Records. Don't push or over-do. Open when your health is good.

Don't open while driving or sleeping.

Operating any type of heavy machinery while your Records are open is physically taxing and dangerous. When your Records are open, the full attention you need while driving is diverted and not fully available. In the same way, sleeping with your Records open is not energetically supportive because you are not consciously available to the flow of the Records. Stationary and fully present are best.

Process:
Open Your Akashic Records

Before you begin, make sure you have the recording of the visualization, the blessing, and these steps of the process. (All available in the Reader's Packet: https://www.cherylmarlene.com/yourown/)

1. Close your eyes.

The flow of the visualization is enhanced and more easily experienced if you close your eyes. If you are using a recording of the visualization, now is the time to start playback.

2. Balance between Heaven and Earth.

This is the visualization. Begin with your tree and safe, comfortable place.

3. Extend your awareness along your path.

The middle portion of the visualization where, after finding balance between heaven and earth, you feel a path extend from your center.

4. When you come to the end of the path at your entryway, open your eyes and say the opening section of the blessing out loud.

You are on the outside of your entryway; you have not gone through yet. Take a deep breath and feel yourself in this moment. Read the blessing out loud, focusing on each word and thought.

5. Re-focus on your entryway, closing your eyes. Breathe deeply and feel yourself move through your entryway.

It is very important that you go all the way through your entryway. Don't stop halfway. Go completely through your entryway.

6. Open your awareness to whatever you experience as you move through your entryway to whatever you find beyond your entryway.

This is the point which will be different for each person. No two people have exactly the same experience. Some see a garden or a forest. Others see nothing yet sense the presence of others. While still other folks do not see or feel anything. Whatever your experience is, it is exactly right for you. The most important point is to not debate with yourself whether this is the Akashic Records. Assume whatever happens for you is your Akashic Records.

7. Say out loud "The Records are open." Feel them open if you haven't already.

It may take several attempts to feel like you are connecting. Don't worry! Take a deep breath, release expectations, and trust yourself. You are now in your Akashic Records.

8. Open your eyes.

Remember: keep your eyes open while you are connected with your Akashic Records.

9. Ask questions and respond as appropriate with all information.

The Masters, Teachers, and Loved Ones of your Akashic

Records want to communicate with you. What happens now is very much like a conversation with a friend. You ask a question and receive a response. If you don't understand the response, ask for clarification just as you would when a friend says something you don't understand. A response may raise up another question. If so, feel free to ask. If they are giving you information quicker than you can take in, ask them to slow down. Don't be afraid to ask a question, to ask for assistance, or to ask for answers to be repeated.

10. When complete say the closing section of the blessing out loud, "In love and light I thank my Masters, Teachers, and Loved Ones for their information and guidance. Amen. Amen. Amen."

In closing your Records, you do not return to the entryway and the path, instead you use Amen. The first Amen brings you out of your Akashic Records. The second brings you past the threshold between spiritual and physical, and the third brings you back into your physical space.

11. Feel the entry close and say out loud "The Records are closed."

Through clear intention, the Records close. Don't worry if information continues to come. This is the residual left in the "hose" or you are continuing to process and understand.

7

EXPERIENCE

I have taught people around the world, in multiple languages, how to open the Akashic Records. Initially, the difficulty is that each person has a different experience when they move through their entryway. As a teacher, I can offer nothing but general guidelines. As a student, you must step into the unknown prepared for any experience, moving beyond expectation or belief.

When I first began teaching, I asked the Records for more clarity, concise steps, and defined experience. Their response was that I was asking for training wheels. In return, they questioned me about the type of teacher I wanted to be and the kind of experience I wanted for my students? They could very easily offer the crutch of specific steps, once past the entry. However, at some point, if I wanted to be a teacher for a student's deepest and highest, I was going to need to take away the training wheels and encourage the student to step into the unknown. They believed that it was in the deepest and highest for me and all my students to accept the challenge in the initial moments rather than delay to some unspecified future.

You are here now to meet this challenge. You may not feel entirely ready, yet now's the time. As I've said to every student before you: trust yourself that now is the time to accept that you can enter your Akashic Records. Whatever *your experience, you will now step forward and claim your path for yourself, without training wheels.*

Ultimately, this is what your life is about: stepping into the unknown, unprepared, beyond expectation, into your deepest and highest.

Accept that now is the time.

What the Akashic Records Are and Aren't

The process of opening the Akashic Records uses a visualization and a blessing and includes an opening and a closing.

There are many forms of knowing; the Akashic Records is one form of knowing. What differentiates the Akashic Records from other forms of knowing is the intention of connecting and entering the Akashic Records.

To open the Akashic Records at the deepest levels possible, you must have a firm foundation which you learn to trust over time. In the beginning, this is how you know you are in the Akashic Records: when you follow the opening process, say the blessing out loud, and go through your entryway—you are in the Akashic Records. Following the closing process and saying the closing part of the blessing, closes the Akashic Records. There may be "drips" after closing or you may continue processing what you received, but this is not a reopening of your Records.

If you don't do the process and say the blessing, you are not in the Akashic Records. You don't spontaneously or automatically open the Akashic Records.

My best advice: Don't debate with yourself. If you follow the process, that's the Akashic Records. You are a beginner, just learning. You do not have enough experience to really know whether or not you are in the Akashic Records To begin, keep it simple. If you follow the process and say the blessing, that's the Akashic Records. When you follow the closing process and say the closing, the Akashic Records are closed.

The process and blessing are there to provide you a firm foundation. And you will need this foundation to deepen your practice and strengthen your connection.

The primary challenge in opening your Akashic Records is trust. Can I trust that I'm really doing this? Can I trust this process? Can I trust what I receive? The process and blessing are foundation and help you develop trust. Don't be tempted to change either the process or the blessing. Instead of shifting the process, allow yourself to focus on your experience of trust, and let this help you let go of anything which gets in your way. Opening for yourself requires that you take care of whatever appears for you so you can find, within, your deepest sense of trust in self. The practices which follow will help you through possible blocks and challenges. Yield to your process and allow experience to help you release and deepen your connection.

For Yourself is Challenging

Learning to open your Akashic Records is, surprisingly, more challenging than opening for another. When you open the Akashic Records, you are holding the sacred space of the Reading, receiving the flow of energy, and transmitting this energy and information as best you can. When you do this for yourself, you add an extra step: allowing the energy flow to help you shift, release, and integrate. To feel confident in yourself, you need practice.

Through All Your Senses

Connecting with the Akashic Records happens through all of your senses.

Often you can hear or see. Sometimes you feel. Occasionally you might even smell or taste. Sometimes you just know. Like learning to drive a car, at first you must think about each step. After some practice, you are down the street without even thinking about stepping on the gas.

Akashic Records Practice

As you go forward you will receive support to develop your practice in the Akashic Records. Practice is simply opening your Akashic Records, asking questions, receiving the energy flow and the responses, and opening to the interaction.

The key: PRACTICE! Quantity is not as important as consistency. Opening your Records once a week, every week is helpful. Opening two or three times this week and nothing for three weeks is less helpful. Life is full and busy. Don't push. Just be as consistent as your life allows.

The Challenge of Your Own Emotions

Most likely you are learning to open your Akashic Records because you want support with your life.

In the beginning asking questions that may have a high emotional impact can be challenging to your confidence in receiving the answers. Emotional questions come with desires or expectations for what the answers could be, should be, might be. There can be anxiety and fear which makes receiving the information from your Akashic Records overwhelming.

You will learn strategies to help strengthen your connection. All the practices which follow in this book are filled with questions that are personal in nature but are generally not questions in which response can be predicted or anticipated.

Asking questions of this nature, especially in the beginning, takes the pressure off and allows you the space to learn about how you receive and connect with the energetic flow of your Akashic Records. As you progress, pairing these questions with more personal questions helps to release any blocks and deepens your connection with the Akashic Records.

Questions Form Your Practice

Everything comes from the Akashic Records through intention. Questions express intention. For this reason, practice in your Akashic Records is usually about asking questions and engaging in a dialogue with your Akashic Records.

Don't worry overly about the form of your question. In whatever form a question is asked, the energy of your intention is embedded within the expression of your words. Fretting about your questions places unnecessary judgment on yourself. Trust yourself. If you find it difficult, then ask your Records for assistance.

Some students worry whether they are taking enough time with the Records. As you begin, you're probably going to be in your Records for a shorter duration than a year from now. A year from now, with continued practice, you will have attuned yourself to the energy of your Akashic Records. As you begin, you will be working to put this all together. I won't be specific about the time it might take because I don't want to create anxiety for you if your experience is different. Ask the question, receive a response, and move on to the next question without putting your eye on the clock—that's the best.

If you don't feel you have questions to ask in your Records, go easy on yourself. When you are beginning, sometimes overwhelming feelings can limit your awareness of questions. That's why this book is filled with questions for you to ask. Give yourself a break and don't be so hard on yourself. All will work out.

Not Always the Same

When you first open your Akashic Records, you have an experience which comes with a certain awareness. Over time, this experience may shift and different awareness may appear. This type of shift is not unusual. What shouldn't change are the components of the process you use to open your Akashic Records. There is always a tree, but maybe not always the same tree. When you go completely through the entryway, what you find may change from opening to opening but there is always an entryway and an experience beyond the entry. Let go of your expectations and open to whatever experience may come for you.

Your Akashic Records Journal

In working in your Akashic Records, usually you engage in a dialogue or conversation with the presence or guides of your Akashic Records. Not only might you forget after a few days but putting energy into remembering can slow the flow of the energy in your Records. The best solution is to write down what you receive.

Enter: Your Akashic Records Journal.

Find a journal to use only for your Akashic Records work. When you are in your Akashic Records, write down as best you can whatever you receive. While the writing creates a record for you, writing also distracts your mind so that your heart is free to do the work. Know you won't get everything down, but what you do record will capture the essence of the flow. If you'd rather, type your notes on your computer.

. . .

Akashic Record Journal Tips:

Find a journal which lays flat to avoid writing on the curve which can happen when the journal is open. Also consider the page thickness if you want to write on both sides.

Begin each day on a new page and record the day and date at the top of the page.

No need to write down your questions. Instead, put short abbreviated notes across the top of the page (above the date). This will help you remember what you want to ask. This also creates a table of contents of sorts, useful when you're trying to find something.

Creating Space

When you learn to open your Akashic Records, you are adding a new opportunity to your life which will take some time and effort to integrate.

In a physical sense, you will need to think about where you open your Records. Generally, you will be inside, perhaps sitting at a desk or table, in a room by yourself. If you live with others, ask for some uninterrupted time alone. Quiet is preferred; no TV or music playing.

In an organizational sense, you will need to open your schedule to find time to work with your Records. This can be challenging. Lives are busy and full. In the beginning, think about one or two times a week which you feel will work for you over time. Of course, this can shift. Yet, starting out with realistic expectations can help the organizational integration happen sooner than later.

In a spiritual sense, you might want to add a bit of ritual to your practice. For example, you might want to light a candle or burn sage to acknowledge the sacred nature of opening. You also may find that holding a piece of quartz or turquoise while opening is helpful. Or having several stones sitting near you. Once you can open your Akashic Records, you can ask for suggestions for both ritual and stones, or other helpful items.

When you open your Akashic Records, the process focuses your attention and supports your connection. While you don't want to become dependent on just the exact, perfect conditions, adding flourishes which support you is ok.

Opening your Records outside is wonderful. Sitting in a forest, on the beach, or wherever you may find yourself is highly recommended. Keep a small notebook with the blessing in your purse or backpack to use outside.

Overall, the best direction is to become confident enough in your connection to open your Akashic Records in the worst scenario, knowing that you may never need to do this. Don't be picky about your ritual, or you might freeze your growth in the Records. Essential: be able to open your Akashic Records anywhere, at any time, regardless of the situation.

After the first time opening, then what?

Once you have opened your Akashic Records, you have two choices before you.

One choice is *no, thank you*. You decide, for some reason, that the Akashic Records are not for you. Whatever your other experiences in life, you come to this process with me as a beginner. Truthfully, once is not enough to pass judgment on yourself or this process. I encourage you to delay this decision until you have tried it again—at least five or six more times. However, I also acknowledge that truth for you may not be the Akashic Records. Following your truth is always the best path.

The second choice is *yes, thank you.* You know that you want to keep going. Perhaps there were some hitches in your first opening, you may have felt strong connection, or experienced something in between. Either way, you are committing to working through what may arise. You are saying yes to yourself, to your journey, to exploring and receiving whatever may come.

After the first time, what is before you is one simple effort: practice. Each time you open your Akashic Records, you are there as a beginner learning in the moment what is offered. Whether it be the second time or the thousandth time, this approach is the same. Remember this is not about practice makes perfect. Instead, each practice is simply repeated effort to explore, learn, and understand. As you practice, you will notice shifts in yourself, in your connection with the Akashic Records, and in the flow of each opening.

8

FIRST OPENING

N ervous? Excited? Uncertain? Confident? A mix of everything? I remember the first time I opened the Akashic Records. I was a mix of emotions including a really big dose of "Oh no! What if it doesn't work? I may not be good enough."

I did the first time what I have done every time since: I put my worry to my side and slightly behind. I said to myself that this is not about "can't," this is about "how I learn". I will not begin from the place of limitation if for no other reason than limitation is not what the Akashic Records are about for me. I will instead stand in my place of possibility, open to whatever the experience may be.

This is all you need to do: be open to whatever comes, however the flow approaches. While it might seem easier for me to tell you exactly what to expect, that would also rob you of the fullness of your personal experience. Rather in a place of limitation, begin opening to all possibility.

Take a deep breath. Where you are in this moment is exactly where you begin. See yourself in a space of possibility and feel your heart open to this possibility. Know that right now failure is simply not making the effort. You can and will open your Akashic Records because that is why you are here, now, for yourself. Another deep breath and feel all of you integrate with this moment.

Now you are ready to begin.

Let's put this all together!

When you open your Akashic Records, you need the following:

- A quiet location where you won't be interrupted
- Pen and Akashic Records Journal (or your computer)
- Your Akashic Records Blessing
- The steps of the process for opening your Akashic Records
- Visualization recording, if using
- Questions or issues to raise (suggested questions are at the end of this chapter)

Remember, your opening process has three components:

- Visualization
- Blessing, and
- Process

Use a recording of the visualization until you feel comfortable on your own. Know where your blessing is and have it with you as you begin the process. The process is not complicated and, for very specific energetic reasons, should to be completed in the order I offer to you.

The steps of the process indicate when to use the visualization and when to say your blessing. Follow the process from start to finish and you will be able to open your Akashic Records.

For your ease, here are the steps of the process:

1. Close your eyes.
2. Balance between Heaven and Earth using the visualization.
3. Extend your awareness along your path.
4. When you come to the end of the path and your entryway, open your eyes and say the opening section of your blessing out loud.
5. Re-focus on your entryway, closing your eyes. Breathe deeply and feel yourself move through your entryway.
6. Open your awareness to whatever you experience as you move through your entryway to whatever you find beyond your entryway.
7. Say out loud "The records are open." Feel them open if you haven't already.
8. Open your eyes.
9. Ask questions and receive all responses as appropriate.
10. When complete, say the closing section of the blessing out loud, "In love and light I thank my Masters, Teachers, and Loved Ones for their information and guidance. Amen. Amen. Amen."
11. Feel the entry close and say out loud "The Records are closed."

First Time!

Use the questions below in your first opening.

In this first time, you will probably only open for five or ten minutes. As you practice more, the opening time will increase.

The biggest block initially may be expecting fully formed sentences which you think you will receive before beginning to write. However, at first, it's most common to receive only several words or a phrase. The flow usually doesn't begin until you begin writing. A great method to begin the flow is writing down, "The answer is ...."

Many people only see images. If that's the case, follow-up with more questions which ask for information about how the image relates to your question. Rely on whatever sense or knowing may come forward for you as you see the image. Also, don't hesitate to draw what you see if only in rough, rudimentary sketches. I don't draw well, but I always make an attempt. Just like words on a page, the images on the page capture the energy of what is being transmitted. Also, for images, I often just describe quickly what I see and mark it in my journal as an image with this tag: [image].

It's common to receive only through your knowing and awareness. If this is the case, don't immediately dismiss what may come to you. Write down what comes even if it just feels like you. Your resistance, analysis, and doubt block and weaken the flow. Openness encourages flow.

No matter the type of response, it's perfectly acceptable to follow-up with more questions to clarify and extend what you receive. Just as speaking with a friend and wanting to understand more clearly or deeply, you simply ask. Expect with more practice, the time you spend in your Records will increase and what you receive will expand. Remember this first time, all you may receive is three or four words per question—and that's great!

Questions for the First Time

Gather what you need. Balance between heaven and earth; at your entryway say the blessing out loud; and then open your Akashic Records. Ask these questions:

1. Why am I learning to open my Akashic Records?
2. What am I here to learn?

9

SECOND OPENING

Congratulations!!

You have stepped forward and made the effort at something new, something different, something for you!

How did your first opening go?

I don't ask this question for you to bring out your critic and judge. Instead, observe and witness your experience. Notice what happened from the moment you thought, "I am going to open my Records" until you said the last Amen of closing. Notice if you felt nervous or unsure and if that feeling shifted as you proceeded with the process. Notice if you felt disbelief or doubt and when these feelings might have arisen. Notice when you felt excited or connected and take stock of what these feelings might have come from.

In other words, don't draw harsh conclusions or judgments. Don't immediately think, "That didn't work" or "I'm not good!" This will slam the door on your ability to move forward.

In this moment, learn! What worked? What didn't? Maybe you didn't record the visualization and now realize that hearing it will help. Maybe you didn't find your entryway, or you skipped the part about your tree and safe, comfortable place.

Make notes to yourself. Next time, I will include all the process. I will breathe. I will write down whatever I receive. I will breathe. I will breathe in the energy of the earth and bring in the energy of the heavens. I will say my blessing out loud. I will give myself a better chance to succeed.

My best advice at this point is don't debate with yourself, don't struggle, don't second guess. Give yourself a chance to take in the new scenery and welcome a new path. You are beginning, new, without long-term experience in this process.

To move forward, complete these sentences for yourself:

In learning to open the Akashic Records, I am thankful for:

To help myself step forward in opening my Akashic Records, I release these expectations:

In claiming trust for myself in this process of learning to open my Akashic Records, I open my heart because:

Second Opening

Take a little break—maybe ten or fifteen minutes. Walk around, go outside if the weather allows. Then re-read the chapter on the process. Re-acquaint yourself with what comes first (your tree and your safe, comfortable place), where you say your blessing out loud (at the entryway at the end of the path), and the words for closing your Records and how you say them.

Look at the questions below. These are the questions you might ask in your second opening.

When you feel ready, take a deep breath and begin.

Gather what you need, open your Akashic Records, and ask these questions:

1. How do I set myself up for failure?
2. How can I claim more happiness for myself in my life?
3. What gets in the way of choice for me?
4. What can I do to improve my connection with my Akashic Records?

If you and I were working one-on-one, this would be the point where I would suggest a break. Let's take a walk, get outside—that kind of break.

If you can't get outside right now, imagine yourself taking a walk with me. See the sun, the trees, the snow, the sky, the aliveness all around. Know you are connected always to this wonderfulness!

Breathe. Relax. Take in what you have been learning.
Ask yourself: What's important for me to acknowledge in this moment?

SECTION II

FOUNDATION

Process creates foundation.

Practice and experience strengthen process.

Trust builds, truth emerges.

As you journey in your Akashic Records:
Honor and respect yourself.

Allow your firm foundation to provide support and knowing.

Step forward in trust, finding joy in your life.

10

SOUL ENERGY DYNAMICS

*A*s I have shared, when my Masters, Teachers, and Loved Ones asked me to begin teaching and sharing. I laughed. I thought they were crazy because I felt I needed more experience. At the time, I couldn't see myself shifting who and what I thought I was.

But they persisted and suggested, in a very guide-like way, that I get over myself. According to them, sharing the Akashic Records was part of my path and I needed to figure that out and get on with it. I thought about this for a while, perplexed, cautious, reluctant.

A bit oblivious to the nature of my Records, I asked a question which I thought would stump them. (Yes, please laugh with me on my obvious moment of forgetting who and what I was dealing with!) My question, "Please explain to me, in a way I can share, how the Akashic Records work?"

Nothing in my Akashic Records classes had covered this topic. Nothing I had read up to that point broached the subject. I thought I was asking the impossible. I was completely wrong! The response changed not only my mind, but also irrevocably changed my life.

In a 45-minute lecture, my Records offered an elegant explanation of the soul energetic dynamics of the Akashic Records, which I refer to as the Circle Diagram. This view from the soul point provides a dynamic way to understand the Akashic Records as a flow of energy. What follows is a summary of the main concepts.

To understand the breadth and depth of the Akashic Records, the beginning is always:

Everything is Energy.
All energy exists on a continuum from potential to form.

Potential   Form

Energy is eternal and infinite, both source and substance, seen and unseen, known and unknowable. Every entity and event emerges first as energy: chairs, rocks, people, light, emotion. All we know, see, hear, taste, smell, and feel is made of energy. We are energy. Energy is the foundation of our boundless universe. Everything is Energy.

In the physical sense, energy is the capacity for motion and the possibility of transferring motion. From a spiritual perspective, energy is the infinite movement of the transcendent awareness present in all. As divine spark, energy is motion within and without.

The Akashic Records are also formed of energy and flow within this infinite and eternal realm. Understanding energy is the first step while energy will, in return, support every step of your journey in the Akashic Records. Attempts are made to understand the Akashic Records without energy, but that is like trying to explain the ocean without understanding the nature and power of water. To understand the Akashic Records, exploration of the fundamentals of energy is the beginning point. Then it is easier to understand how the Akashic Records flow within and utilize the natural characteristics and abilities of energy.

Energy flows on a continuum from potential to form.

Energy exists on a continuum with potential on one end and form at the other. Energy is always in motion along this continuum. All energy is either potential, form, or part of the flow somewhere in between.

The energy continuum is neither two nor three dimensional; it is infinite and eternal. Each point of the continuum is the timeless Now, with infinite possibility for the next Now. Both hard to imagine and hard to draw, the energy flow on every point of the continuum is in an infinite number of directions, spiraling through the infinity of experience and form. In the still point between moments is the infinite possibility of potential available to express as form.

Potential is the vast possibility of the universe intrinsic within energy. Potential, allied with intention, steps forward from the great unknown, becoming source for realizing this moment of desire and dream, this moment of being and becoming.

Form is the creative manifestation of potential's intention. As potential moves along the continuum to form, intention grows steadily, until potential becomes its desired form. All energy repeats this eternal cycle: potential flowing to form, then releasing as form, energy returning to potential.

While the acorn may not fall far from the mighty oak, both acorn and oak are expressions of potential and of form. Energy is potential. Energy is form. Energy is the journey.

The continuum of energy exists within All That Is. All That Is encompasses all known, unknown, and unknowable and contains both chaos and order, forever beyond, and yet eternally within.

All That Is is described as a box, not because that is what it is, but because the lines of the box illustrate the limits of knowing. There is much that may never be consciously known beyond the edges of the box. All That Is: everything inside *and* outside the box.

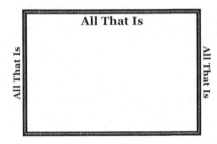

Words cannot encompass the indescribable totality of All That Is. The mind cannot comprehend the whole, only parts, while the heart can feel connection with the eternal essence of All That Is.

Energy exists as either wave or particle

Wave is a physical description of the dynamic, infinite, timeless ebb and flow of energy. Potential moves as waves across the entirety of All That Is.

As a particle, energy is a fixed focus of individual awareness, capable of expressing the intention of its potential. Particle begins the awareness of I and other, of subject and object, allowing energetic flow towards form.

Gather what you need, open your Akashic Records, and ask these questions:

1. How does my intention realize form from my soul's potential?
2. How can I connect with the awareness of my soul's wave state?
3. What message do my Masters, Teachers, and Loved Ones have for me today?

11

SOUL ORIGIN

P owerful support comes from seeing beyond belief. Just when we think we know, a new idea steps forward and issues challenge. I used to freeze, holding myself back from these new vistas. One day, I realized that freezing was a habit which no longer served me. Using affirmations and support from my Akashic Records, as well as my friends, I let go of the habit. Now I look forward to stepping into shift and seeing with new eyes.

Our world is changing, and I don't want to be stuck in the habit of avoiding new ideas. I step forward in trust, without fear, open to receive the offered newness. The following includes new ideas. Please thoughtfully consider this before rejecting something as wrong simply because it is new.

Within All That Is, are two arenas of energetic experience:

Non-Physical Reality and Physical Reality

Non-Physical Reality, an ocean of pure potential, is the origin of the unknowable and the ineffable of divine source. Filled with wave after wave of potential, Non-Physical Reality exists beyond form, beyond the quantum potential, within the origins of All That Is.

Emerging from that point on the energy continuum where energy is more form than potential (the quantum potential), Physical Reality includes all expression of form from the daintiest photon to dense, consolidated physical forms such as planets, stars, and the human body.

Resistance is the motion of energy which assists in refining and clarifying intention to define form. Because resistance exists in Physical Reality but not in Non-Physical Reality, energy flows from Non-Physical Reality to Physical Reality in order to satisfy intention and manifest form.

At some moment, a wave in Non-Physical Reality realizes that it is an individual wave among an infinite number contained within All That Is and begins its journey from potential to form following intention. In this moment of self-realization, the wave becomes particle. As a focus of intention, this particle, still within Non-Physical Reality, is called the Soul Point. The Soul Point is the soul's origin and the focus of individual awareness.

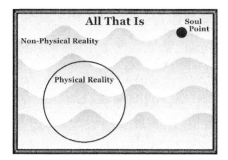

In the moment the soul realizes its individual nature, the soul also consciously realizes that the whole of All That Is exists and wants to participate. The soul sends intention into Physical Reality to manifest form looking to find an anchor within one of the many expressions of form available within Physical Reality. To be on Earth, the soul responds to the intention Earth sends to help the soul follow intention and create form.

The intention of the soul joining with the intention of the earth joins and anchors the spiritual with the physical. The connection of these intentions creates an energetic spark which produces the Human Energy Field. Within this field the human body takes form receiving soul intention and Earth's knowledge of physical form.

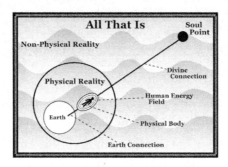

With you always, the connection between Soul Point and Human Energy Field, your Divine Connection, is eternal and unbreakable. The spiritual journey leads to a discovery of this connection, revealing the expression of divinity within. At physical death, when the physical anchor releases, Divine Connection becomes the path home to soul's origin—the Soul Point.

In the same way, connection with the Earth cannot be destroyed. From the Earth Connection, comes the physical stability of the human body, knowledge of the basic physical laws governing Earth, as well as the agreements of human existence. With awareness of this powerful link comes the deep feelings of expansive connection with the natural world and the fullness of physical being. The growing awareness of physical connection to Earth brings awareness of deeper spiritual possibilities. When the time comes to return fully as potential to Soul

Point, Earth gently releases her intention of holding space on Earth, freeing form to return to potential at the Soul Point.

The energy of the Akashic Records is accessed at the Soul Point.

Each person's Akashic Record exists within the energy of the Soul Point and Non-Physical Reality. Eternal and infinite in character, the Akashic Records are beyond time and space, holding the promise of potential and the opportunity of form. Rather than a physical body viewpoint, through the Akashic Records the perspective is from the soul's point of view.

To enter the Akashic Records, extend awareness outside of the physical body, beyond the Human Energy Field, and "travel" past the resistance of Physical Reality, through Divine Connection and the pure potential of Non-Physical Reality to the Soul Point.

Connection in the Akashic Records does not happen with only one point of contact. Instead, the Akashic Records are a collective experience where there is soul to soul connection with the many and the One both as dialogue and as meditative integration.

Opening the Akashic Records is also an experience unique for each individual. The flow of energy comes to everyone differently depending on intention, expectation, and need. Most often, the flow of energy feels like a conversation with others.

In the Akashic Records, the others are called the Masters, Teachers and Loved Ones and surround the Soul Point. Truly it does not matter exactly who the others are because these guides, these keepers, are drawn forward by the individual in the moment of expressing intent. In the Akashic Records, the Masters, Teachers, and Loved Ones don't dictate; they guide and are present as the reflectors, the witnesses, and the supporters of personal process.

- The Loved Ones identify unlimited soul-to-soul connection.
- Teachers are the energy of guidance and learning, reminders of the possibility of moving beyond outmoded boundaries of yesterday.
- Masters transcend the individual and call forth the possibilities of alignment with the boundlessness and the divine.

The Masters, Teachers and Loved Ones are also a soul's soul group. Though they may not appear when entering the Akashic Records, they receive intention and transmit responses in alignment with highest expression. Each person will have a different group of Guides, which may appear to shrink or expand over time because this group flows with the needs of the soul and body in each moment and across all moments. Additionally, the Masters, Teachers and Loved Ones usually stay nameless because they are not present for their own personal desires. They are responding as witnesses to the intentions of the soul they are invited to attend. Each opening of the Akashic Records is a unique moment of the attention offered by the Masters, Teachers and Loved Ones.

Gather what you need, open your Akashic Records, and ask these questions:

1. How may I strengthen my connection in the Akashic Records with my soul point?
2. What resistance do I have to understanding Non-Physical Reality?
3. Do I have any beliefs which interfere with clear interaction with Non-Physical Reality?
4. What message do my Masters, Teachers, and Loved Ones have for me today about soul energy dynamics?

12

ENERGETIC EXPRESSION

The moment the Akashic Records told me of the dynamic view, I knew my life had been irrevocably impacted, forever shifted. Here I introduce a concept I will explain in depth later. Start with this simple taste, allowing the energy represented by the words to slowly raise your awareness to the monumental shift which will come. The new shift on the planet is all about how we understand the dynamic nature of All That Is. Remember, it's a case of not one or the other—but both.

Energy can be understood from both a static/linear point of view and a dynamic or infinite and eternal point of view.

The standard perception holds motion within three-dimensional space and views time as a straight line through a chronology of past, present, and future. This is the static view, limited to the linear.

Moving beyond linear boundaries, space becomes infinite in dimension and time is eternal within the dynamic view. In the dynamic view, time is not a straight line. Instead, time flows infinitely and eternally from this moment like a fountain outward in the 360 degrees of a sphere. Rather than a chronology of events connected linearly, in the dynamic view each moment now is connected through awareness of this present moment with the next. When freed from a linear perspective, energetic motion is perceived as random or chaotic from the static view.

The Akashic Records exist in Non-Physical Reality, outside of linear time, firmly within the dynamic view. Entering the Akashic Records is to see from the soul's point of view which is decidedly neither linear nor three-dimensional. The dynamic view completely shifts the energetic understanding of the Akashic Records. No longer confined to explanations from the static view, possibility and capacity expand.

For example, understood dynamically, the concept of memory is very different. Within the static view, memory is awareness of what happened in the past—what is remembered. Within the dynamic view, memory is awareness of connection between this moment and all moments, lifting perceptions into the infinite and eternal.

Opening the Akashic Records to ask a question, intention brings forward knowing within this moment. The knowing is not static and neither recorded nor retrieved from linear time.

Additionally, all energy flows within the dynamic view and allows understanding of the Akashic Records to be more than what is perceived within the static view. No longer limited to library and book, or past life information, the Akashic Records yield knowing as a dynamic connection in this moment between the soul and human awareness.

Energy's movement is resonance

Experience in the Akashic Records comes in many forms. One aspect is the awareness of motion which usually begins gently and expands as practice progresses.

The static view of energy focuses on vibration. The two linear components of vibration are frequency (how often motion is repeated) and amplitude (the peaks and valleys of energy within three-dimensional space).

Through the dynamic view, energy is about resonance. Resonance is the resounding or reverberation of energy throughout the infinite and eternal and within the potential of the moment across all aspects body, mind, heart and soul. Resonance is not confined or limited by vibration. Resonance searches for affinity, balance, and connection between seemingly separate flows of energy where separation is no longer perceived because all flows are in balance one with the other.

Gather what you need, open your Akashic Records, and ask these questions:

1. What can I do to receive deeper awareness and understanding of the dynamic view?
2. How can my awareness of this world shift from vibration to resonance?
3. What message do my Masters, Teachers, and Loved Ones have for me today?

13

UNIVERSAL CO-CREATION

Spiritual becomes physical through the interaction of three Co-Creative Universal Forces.

The soul's intention initiates energy flow on the continuum from potential to form yielding physical manifestation. Intention interacts with the animative force of the universe in a co-creative dance. Tempering and expanding the intention, the dance to go beyond finds alignment and resonance with the highest and deepest expression of the soul in this moment. Three motions interact and yield the co-creation of humanity.

1. Spiritual Inheritance—everything which the soul brings as the soul it is.
2. Physical Inheritance—everything which the physical body brings including the physical and spiritual legacy of the biological parents.
3. Universal Life Force—creative, divine movement dynamically animating the spiritual and physical into multi-dimensional expressions of energy.

The interaction of spiritual and physical creates a point on a timeline. The interaction of Universal Life Force is what turns this interaction into a multi-dimensional human being.

The interaction of these co-creative forces makes physical experience on the Earth. Without any one of these three motions, physical form on this Earth would not be possible.

In the Akashic Records, balance with these three universal forces is always present. Balance already exists, it does not need to be created. Balance only requires coming to awareness of its eternal, unbreakable existence within the integration of spiritual and physical with Universal Life Force.

Gather what you need, open your Akashic Records, and ask these questions:

1. What is the nature of my spiritual inheritance?
2. What is the nature of my physical inheritance?
3. Am I in resistance to Universal Life Force? Why?
4. What message do my Masters, Teachers, and Loved Ones have for me today about universal co-creation?

14

ENERGY CHARACTERISTICS

*T*he three characteristics of energy was another concept which astonished me. As much as I have delved into the implications of this knowledge, there is much more to learn. Below I introduce each characteristic and, in the next three lessons, offer deeper exploration.

Energy has three characteristics: motion, intention and knowing.

Any flow of energy contains all three characteristics, because one cannot exist without the other two. The quality or essence of the three can differ between physical forms but all three characteristics appear within all flows of energy.

- **Motion is shift, change.**

  Energy is always in motion: movement; animation; bringing to life; creative spark. From motion comes the perception of space as both a finite, defined form (which can be measured) and an infinite, boundless form (that cannot be measured).

- **Intention is desire for experience**.

As the focused internal urge to participate, intention gives direction to motion. Intention helps step into and unveil the mystery of All That Is. Clarity of intention opens the door to observe experience and make choice about how to respond or participate. Intention is not about a specific end. Rather, intention is a focus on the desire of experience in this moment, which may shift in any moment of the journey.

- **Knowing is how to know**.

Arising from potential, knowing is a process of becoming aware of what can be known. In contrast, information is the content or form produced by this process. Knowing is the witness of motion. Appearing just before awareness happens, motion sparks awareness and begins the process of knowing.

When knowing as a personal process is compromised, personal truth is sought outside of self from the outer master, someone who will offer another form of truth. The inner master is an inner source of truth, within the heart, and is supported by a clear process of knowing. Beginning inside, the inner master brings awareness of inner truth through personal knowing.

Gather what you need, open your Akashic Records, and ask these questions:

1. What do my Masters, Teachers, and Loved Ones have to share in this moment about the three characteristics of energy?
2. Why do the three characteristics always come together in energy?

15

MOTION

C ast your eyes to the ocean. Watch the water. Feel the water. Observe. What do you receive?

Take a deep breath. Smell. Taste the air. Again, what do you receive?

Motion. You receive motion. Motion is both what you receive and how you receive.

The ocean is motion. Whether as the swell of wave, the approach to shore, or a drop of water, the ocean is always in motion.

Your awareness of the ocean is motion. Through all your senses, through observation and the flow of your knowing, motion is what connects and carries that which is flowing within your awareness and knowing, consciously or unconsciously. In whatever manner you engage with the world, the engagement is powered by motion. Motion delivers. Motion is what creates a flow of energy and is the means by which all energy flows.

For your mind, motion behaves as both noun and verb, as both name and action. Motion makes interaction work as evident flow. Amplified, motion hits peaks and sinks to valleys.

Motion powers the static flow of past, present, and future. Motion also elevates awareness to absorb the dynamic possibility of the infinite and the eternal.

Motion propels self. And, self seeks motion's progress. Motion ignites heart, activates mind, and exercises body. Soul motion sings, turning life into dance and self into song.

Arising from the boundless, motion is defined as animating force created by the transcendent energy of All That Is.

Motion is ignited by first breath entering the eternal return until last breath.

In the stillness is the gathering of motion, not an absence—rather an emerging of the unknowable of All That Is.

Look to youself. Feel. Observe. Witness you.

You are motion experiencing motion, creating motion, living in motion. Honor your motion.

Gather what you need, open your Akashic Records, and ask these questions:

1. How does motion show up in my life?
2. Do I have any beliefs which do not serve me with regard to motion?
3. Show me the motion of my soul point.
4. How is the motion of my soul point connected to all soul points?
5. What is the motion of All That Is?

16

INTENTION

Within the infinite and eternal of this moment, feel harmony and balance at your center. Intention is the desire to feel balance in this moment. Whatever words you use, whatever feelings may arise, intention seeks balance with your truth and All That Is.

Intention becomes guide, becomes direction, becomes your path as you step forward to meet the possibility of this moment. Intention becomes desire, becomes passion, becomes longing as you aim for balance and harmony within.

Yet desire can easily move outside of truth distracted by the illusion of promise. Follow this path and crash into emptiness, devoid of balance, lacking truth.

Stop and consider: is this a different road, one where desire of something is wrong? Yet, this denial is also a vacuum, empty of balance, lacking truth. You are not an empty vessel.

Come back to this moment where desire is the urge, the intention of balance with All That Is, where truth guides you and harmony exists. Find that the road to clear intention is not about the "what" outside, but the "how" inside. Banishing desire disconnects intention from the motion of life.

The joy of desire, focused in truth, receives the joy of intention in balance with you—and All That Is.

In this moment, now, your joyous desire expresses balanced and powerful intention moving you toward your next intention, your next point of balance. With intention, be here, now.

Gather what you need, open your Akashic Records, and ask these questions:

1. How does desire, as an outside enticement, block my path?
2. How do I block my sense of inner joy?
3. Help me feel within my joy as an expression of harmony with All That Is.
4. How can I clarify my intention in each moment?
5. What is my intention today?

17

KNOWING

Knowing comes to you, in the moment of your need, to aid your decisions and support your choices. Neither knowing nor information comes to relieve you of your responsibility for yourself. Rather, knowing comes when you agree that, before all else, you are responsible for your own life, the choices you make, and the path you walk.

Knowing in this expanded perspective is not just the intellectual workings of the mind. Knowing, as the flow of energy, is held within all aspects of mind and heart, body and soul.

Knowing comes in many forms including those we often do not willingly recognize. Emotions, thoughts, and feelings emerge from your knowing, conveying information. More challenging is the recognition that delays, distractions, and deceptions are also vital forms of information for you, flowing as they do from divine knowing.

The infinite flow of energy affects the flow of energy infinitely, creating a dynamic, eternal, reciprocal system of feedback. In each moment, All That Is is firmly concentrated with focused attention toward the realization of your potential's highest expression. Simultaneously, it is providing you with indications about the directions and possibilities of your soul within this amazing creative flow. As you take in your knowing in all its forms, you add your own unique spark, creating new energy, new knowing, and thus new information combining with All That Is to create the possibility of each next moment.

Beliefs, perceptions, and stories are all interpretations of this universal flow of energy as well as additional forms of information. They are the translations you make for yourself to understand the knowing contained within the infinite flow of energy living within you. As creative impulses of this energetic flow, you also possess the awareness of energy and are able to utilize this awareness for your efforts to be an active participant in All That Is.

As you move along the continuum of energy, you transform your perspective of information from static fact to dynamic knowing. Knowing rises above the world of matter, uniting physical with spiritual. You embrace the entirety of your being as your source of knowing.

Knowing is the experience of energy moving within the energetic motion of your soul. Knowing is the guide for your path, while information is the result. Information leads to knowing. Knowing leads to the possibilities of All That Is. Knowing is the awareness of motion within All That Is and within all of you.

Knowing is your awareness of life.

Gather what you need, open your Akashic Records, and ask these questions:

1. How do I stand in the way of my knowing?

2. Do I feel more comfortable being aware of my thoughts, emotions, or body sense? Why?
3. What do I feel in my center?
4. What needs to be cleared at my center to help expand my knowing?
5. What is the truth of my knowing today?

18

TRUST

W hen I first began opening my own Records, I didn't trust myself to receive "correctly." I also realized this lack of trust extended into all parts of my life. My Akashic Record teachers did not address that personal shift, and change was an expected outcome of working with the Records. Focused on how to get information, they hadn't covered the bigger issue of how this would affect me.

In hindsight, I recognize a trust crisis. Everyone goes through this challenge because, at some point, everyone questions trust within their experience in the Akashic Records. The lack of trust may be aimed at yourself, at the process, at me, at what you receive, at the Records, or at whatever your sense of divine transcendence might be.

Trust emerges as belief from reliability. As a beginner, limited in experience with the Akashic Records, I didn't feel either strong belief or solid reliability. Initially, when a response sounded like me, I didn't have enough experience to decide whether it was just me or truly from the Akashic Records. Frustrated and confused, several times I thought of throwing in the towel.

Now, I am very glad I didn't—throw the towel in, that is. Despite my trouble with trust, I realized I was connecting with a deep awareness of my truth, and I was receiving much more than information. Even if this experience was only me, the effort was making a difference in how I understood myself and my life. Though I could not clearly explain my experience or find someone who could, I decided I would keep going. I would get out of my own way, let go of expectation, and open beyond the push to control.

Developing trust in the Akashic Records comes from experience, in incremental amounts over time. For each person a different experience, a different pace, a separate rhythm. Not knowing exactly how or when, one moment trust seems fleeting or inconsistent and in the next moment solid and dependable. Letting go of expectation, allowing whatever will flow within your Akashic Records experience, is the path to trust. In this moment you might feel trust, and in the next moment trust may desert you. You may blame yourself, reject yourself, and say I can't do this. As time passes something inside you shifts, and you feel a call to try again.

Or, you may feel nothing from the first time to the tenth time. And then in a last-ditch attempt, something clicks, and you feel a strong connection and clarity which had been missing.

Your experience is your experience. You do not need anyone to tell you exactly how it should be. Instead, be gentle with yourself. Don't jump to immediate or irrevocable decisions about what is and isn't true about your connection with the Akashic Records. Through practice, give yourself the opportunity to learn to discern the difference between you and your Akashic Records. Experience, over time, will make a huge difference and is the only way to learn.

As you continue your journey, you will find ways to assess and release blocks through practice. Take advantage of all that is offered, and you will create space for yourself. You will also develop trust simply by the gentleness you bring forward for yourself through your practice.

Gather what you need, open your Akashic Records, and ask these questions:

1. What is trust for me?
2. What will help me trust my experience in the Akashic Records?
3. What are the biggest obstacles to trusting myself?
4. What beliefs do I have that get in my way of trust?
5. What is my truth today about trust?

19

TRUTH

*B*ecause *I trust myself, I am comfortable with hearing and receiving my truth. Your journey in the Akashic Records begins with learning trust. As trust becomes firmer, you open to hearing your truth because you trust yourself. Trust leads to truth, leads to a new level of trust and a greater awareness of truth... a spiral path, ever-evolving, ever-expanding, always supporting.*

Truth. What is truth in the Akashic Records?

Focusing on the Akashic Records as a source of information, then truth might be verifiable. This would be a form of objective truth or a truth that is true for all people regardless of culture or perception. For example, water freezes at a certain temperature. Or the earth revolves around the sun. These are truths that are objective, verifiable. However, the Akashic Records are not limited to objective truth.

The Akashic Records, especially when experienced as knowing, healing, and spiritual practice, are more than objective, they are also subjective. This means that truth is in the eye of the beholder. What is true for you may not be true for me. And, only you can clearly identify what is truth for you.

Truth resonates within you, coming from the balance of who you are in this moment. This experience of truth means that what is true today may not be true tomorrow. You are who you are in the moment, and from this moment you will have new experiences, learn, and grow. In the next moment, tomorrow, next week, you will be a different person than you are in this moment. What you feel as truth in this moment may be significantly different, or barely noticeably different, than what resonates as truth for you a month from now.

I, along with many of my students, have struggled with truth. One of my best students, in her first Reading, asked, "How can I know what you say is true? How can you prove your words as truth?" A reasonable request, yet one which emerges from the idea that truth must be provable to be truth. I felt urgency in her request. She needed a yardstick to measure truth. She wanted to know with certainty and expected that I could deliver truth and its provable measure.

The yardstick I offered surprised her, "Truth does not need to be provable by outside sources to be valid. You are the yardstick of your truth. Your truth resonates within you. That's how you know your truth. You listen, receive, and check your response within your heart and mind and body. That's why you have them, among other reasons, to help you filter and ascertain resonance."

She struggled with these words. She is a very bright, rational, productive person accustomed to weighing information through a logical, intellectual process of deniable proof. Yet something clicked, in an unexpected place, within her. She took a deep breath, and I felt her shift her awareness from outside to inside. Yes, she still had resistance; yet she had given herself a new opportunity to consider, to move deeper, and expand her life.

"In other words," she said, "You are saying that if I trust myself, I can know my truth." Yes, exactly! On your journey, truth is for you to recognize. Trust creates the opening for you to enter your heart and hear your truth. This was a pivotal point of deep significance for this student and profoundly shifted her life and helped her to balance the demands of logical thought with the gentle awareness of inner knowing of truth.

Like this student, when I first began my journey in the Akashic Records, I didn't understand this difference. I struggled to understand whether what I was receiving was verifiable or not. Or, if some other type of truth—whatever that might be—was part of my experience, could it be proven? There were several experiences which came together to help me understand the concept of truth in the Akashic Records, and the most important involved a question.

In my late twenties and early thirties, I was fortunate to have an incredible doctor in my life. A naturopath by training, she was also a medical intuitive who offered great support in releasing much that didn't serve me. During one of my sessions, we began speaking about the nature of truth. She told me that the most important truth for me to understand was my own, in this moment. I felt a thrill of understanding rise in me and knew that I had just heard my truth. I thought about this all the way home—which at the time was a two-hour drive.

The next morning, I sat down at my desk and opened my Akashic Records. I asked, "What is my truth today?" The response shook me to my core, filled my heart with joy, and helped me release a huge load of no-longer-helpful beliefs. I spent my day in both excited awareness and stunned perception. The next morning, I repeated the question, "What is my truth today?" Again, the response hit home with powerful awareness, though what I received was completely different from the first asking. I continued for several weeks, asking this question each time I opened my Records. By about the tenth time, I didn't have to ask the question because as soon as I opened, my Records were already answering the question for me. This began a ritual that I continue to this day.

This one question significantly shifted my experience of the Akashic Records. After asking all these years, I still cannot predict the answer. Each time I ask, I receive a different response based on who I am in the moment. This has helped me understand the process of truth in the Akashic Records.

I can now ask highly-charged emotional and personal questions and HEAR the response without expectation, blame, fear, or judgment intruding. My expectations about objective truth in the Akashic Records have disappeared. Not about outward verification, the point is how I understand what resonates with me and why. Most importantly: I do not need outside validation for my truth.

What is my truth today? Please include this powerful question within your Akashic Records practice. This one question will shift your life.

Gather what you need, open your Akashic Records, and ask these questions:

1. How do I recognize truth?
2. How am I not truthful with myself?
3. How am I not truthful with others?
4. What is my truth today?

20

CLEANSING

A clear channel of connection exists between you and All That Is. The power of this breath brings you to this moment where awareness of connection and balance is possible. This awareness of connection and the feeling of balance are the truths of your being. Truth is most keenly felt in your heart. Finding and listening to your truth becomes the purpose of life.

Cleansing is the process of clearing away that which makes it hard to experience authentic self, to hear truth, and to feel balance. Cleansing is not a destination, rather a journey of spirit. Cleansing constantly renews self, bringing awareness of new clutter, new opportunities to clear, to unburden, to more easily embrace this breath, this moment. Cleansing lightens your load, helping you to let go of blocks and obstacles. Cleansing is responsibility for self, stepping forward, laying claim to the fullest expression of you.

Look around you, where you live, work, and play. What hangs on, begging to be let go? What have you piled on yourself that brings no benefit to you, in this moment? Unfinished projects, unread books, piles of mail? Let them go. Finish, complete, let go.

Cleansing is commitment. Commitment begins with self-honesty. All the unfinished business around you is broken promises in need of cleansing. Broken promises to others, broken promises to yourself - begin cleansing, now.

Cleanse the forgotten and neglected... boxes and piles, stashes and storage long ignored and disregarded. Cleansing makes room, makes space for the new door to open and new opportunity to approach.

Everything you need moves toward you quickly and easily—especially when the path is not boxed in or piled high with stuff and more stuff. Cleansing clears your path, making it easier for you to receive, making it easier for you to hear, making it easier to be, to find you and your truth.

Cleansing encourages a new you, a real you, to step forward. Let go, move on, let be. Cleanse the dust, the ragged edges, the neglected corners of your life. Cleanse the torn, the hastily repaired, the unstable.

In this moment, cleanse, let go.

With this breath, cleanse, let go.

Cleanse you. Uncover your truth and this moment's commitment to you.

Gather what you need, open your Akashic Records, and ask these questions:

1. What in my life is hampered by a lack of commitment?
2. What in my life stands in the way of hearing my truth?
3. What is my personal process for cleaning up a broken promise?
4. How can I improve my ability to complete my commitments?
5. What needs cleansing today?

21

CLAIMING

All That Is is infinite possibility at each and every point of time and space. As you live, each moment of your life passes through, exists within this eternal infinite possibility. In each moment you chose your possibility. You lay claim to infinite possibility. You choose your way, your direction, your path within the boundlessness of All That Is.

Each breath is a claim. Each decision is a claim. Each resistance, each worry, each fear is your claim on eternal possibility. You assert, you don't back down, you come from truth.

Each claim is yours, each claim is your becoming. Each claim is being.

You flow from one claim to another as you understand, or seek to understand, the claims you have made. Looking back on your life, you attempt to explain claims in terms of past events.

Pointed backward in life toward the past there is no clear satisfaction because understanding comes not from how the present moved from the past but how the present moves to the future. Understanding your claims comes from the motion forward toward a greater understanding of self as it becomes comfortable in the eternal ebb and flow of All That Is.

Ask and it shall be given according to the flow of your claim within the dynamic co-creative forces of the universe.

Your asking lays claim, your indecision lays claim, and your response to claim moves from the infinite perspective of All That Is: A perspective you can feel, yet a perspective you cannot see in its entirety.

Trust is the requirement. Trust your sense of truth as you experience in each moment the claim you have made for yourself.

Fear not for you are not alone though your vision may attempt to deceive you. The claim you make now is perfect in its direction and intent. Yet, like all of the universe, your claim is dynamic and quite capable of change. Claim may feel static and unmoving, but that is only your fear seeping through.

You, within your truth and sense of alignment, always have the infinite possibility of new claim, new choice, new direction in this moment and forever. Neither demand nor request, simply assert what is true for you.

Claim yourself today.

Gather what you need, open your Akashic Records, and ask these questions:

1. Describe "claim" for me.
2. How does my past hold me back?
3. How can I learn to trust my truth?
4. How can I live in this moment future-forward?
5. What claims are available to me today?

22

THIS BREATH

Take a deep breath in.

Release it slowly.

Take another deep breath, releasing it slowly.

With each inhale, draw in the support of the universe. Maybe only felt as the physical inhaling of oxygen, but this breath comes to you in its journey from potential to form.

No single breath can be until you decide to engage with the universe. This breath is you stepping into the creative motion of the divine. This breath is you responding to the deepest urges to become an active part of All That Is.

Yes, this breath is a physical requirement. But this breath is not just a physical necessity. This breath also animates your spiritual being. Without this breath you would lack any ability, any intention, any desire to participate in this universe of ours. With this breath you find the courage to step out, to risk, to find out about yourself and your place and potential within the glorious world around you.

Hear clearly: this breath is you on the brink of exploration and discovery. This breath is you staking your claim for the beautiful potential that is you. This breath is the wonder of you. This breath is your wonder meeting the wonder of the universe. Like the next drop of water to take the leap over the waterfall, like the next drop of water that encourages a flower to bloom, this breath is your potential to blossom and thrive. Air is just air. Air only becomes breath when you inhale in this moment, this breath.

This breath, as it draws up inside you, brings nourishment — the nourishment you need for your dreams to become reality, for your fears to release, for your power to find its expression. This breath brings the energy for creation, for expansion, for understanding. This breath brings life force connecting you with the fullness and wonder of the universe. This breath takes in all you need to be you, fully and completely, with the promise of unending potential and the connected expression of All That Is.

On the exhale, you release your fears, your blocks, your disappointments for the unending promise of more support, more clarity, more understanding. Letting go of this breath is the ultimate sign of trust. Letting go of this breath, you signify to yourself the power of the continuous infinite flow of the universe. Form of this breath flowing through this exhale returns to dynamic potential. This breath flows and returns for you again and again as this breath. Each return comes not because of any accomplishment or feat on your part. Each return of this breath flows to you because you are willing to take in this breath.

Breathe in.

Breathe out.

In comes your acceptance and willingness to take part in this amazing moment.

Out happens because of your trust and your understanding.

Breathe in.

Breathe out.

This breath is the universe.

This Breath is you.

Gather what you need, open your Akashic Records, and ask these questions:

1. What can I do to make my breathing easier, more fluid?
2. What can I do to find more support from "This Breath"?
3. When I think of breathing, what do I fear?
4. Is there anything for me to know or understand about "This Breath" that will increase or improve my connection with the Akashic Records?

Break time!
What a journey you are embracing as you explore your Akashic Records.

Put this all away for a bit and allow your experience to integrate.

Reflect on your learning, allowing new awareness to step forward.

Move, breathe, engage with the beauty of this world with an open heart.

SECTION III

CREATE YOUR PRACTICE

Once learned, practice maintains your path of learning, supporting:

Learn Always!

Practice is your choice and your responsibility.

To find your deep road in the Akashic Records:

Practice.

23

PRACTICE

P ractice: action, proficiency, habit. In the process of learning about your Akashic Records and working to establish and maintain connection, you practice. Practice is taking action, stepping in and making an effort instead of viewing at arms-length, from the arm chair of life. Practice is direct, personal engagement.

Practice is also about developing proficiency, exploring capacity, and expanding ability over time. With the Akashic Records, practice is not about getting better in a judgmental few. Rather the Akashic Records is a practice which takes you deeper into potential and into the expansive qualities of divine knowing in this moment. As a journey of unlimited possibility, proficiency is facility and dexterity unhampered by the boundaries of the linear or the static.

Practice overtime supports the development of habit, an expression of a firm foundation. Your process practiced overtime helps you identify what works, what's challenging, and what can be released. It is a continual learning process which improves proficiency and creates a nuanced, subtle, yet flexible habit.

As I've shared, your practice in the Akashic Records is based on the questions you ask and the issues you raise. You will find a way to record what you receive in a journal or on your computer. Asking and recording are the two major activities of your practice though they fuel your learning, your contemplation, and your reflection. In this way, your practice becomes interactive, growing and evolving within the inherent experience and connection shared with the Akashic Records.

To develop a deep connection through practice there are several necessary elements. First, you learn about the nature of the Akashic Records. Already you have learned about soul energy dynamics and soon you will consider a brief history of the Akashic Records as well as three important definitions. A strong practice will also come by digging deeper into the dynamic view and the static view, into choice and responsibility, and into consistency and timing.

Akashic Records practice is driven by intention and the questions you ask. I have some suggestions for pursuing dialogue with your Masters, Teachers, and Loved Ones. While I offer many questions you may choose to ask, ultimately the goal is to put together a practice in the Akashic Records which supports your calling and your desire for connection with the incredible depth and breadth of the Akashic Records.

Your practice will not be static; instead, your experience will evolve over time as you become more proficient, engaged, and confident. Moving beyond linear judgments of good or bad, allow yourself to find dynamic truthful expression of you in this moment. Practice which strives and grows within the power of your spiritual and physical integration will resonate within your body, mind, heart and soul.

. . .

Gather what you need, open your Akashic Records, and ask these questions:

1. How am I open to developing a dynamic practice in the Akashic Records?
2. What stands in my way to full commitment to this dynamic practice?
3. What will help me fully commit to my Akashic Records practice?
4. How do I begin?

24

SPIRITUAL PRACTICE

S imply, spiritual practice is a journey of truth: to find truth within yourself, with the people around you, and in the events forming your life.

Spiritual practice can look like meditating or chanting, going to church, the mosque, and the temple. Spiritual practice includes prayer and song, yoga and dance. Spiritual practice can also include many activities not usually associated with faith and religion, such as quilting, walking, scrubbing floors, washing the dishes, ironing, hauling garbage, waiting tables, and raking leaves.

Spiritual practice is a process of living in which the intention of experiencing spiritual and physical integration guides all experience and action. Spiritual practice connects meaning within your awareness and within the day-to-day experience of living life.

Opening the Akashic Records supports and empowers your efforts to find integration of spiritual and physical within the flow of divine creation. Both as a flow of knowing and a conduit for healing, the Akashic Records facilitates the experience of spiritual practice.

As spiritual practice, one must approach the Akashic Records with the same level of intention and integrity necessary for any spiritual practice. Within the flow of energy, the Akashic Records shines light on truth, choice, and wisdom for you to access and utilize throughout the entire experience of your life. The Akashic Records support all spiritual practice however that practice may appear within your life.

Gather what you need, open your Akashic Records, and ask these questions:

1. What does spiritual practice mean for me?
2. What keeps me from trusting my truth?
3. What expectation, blame, fear, or judgment blocks my ability to integrate spiritual with physical?
4. What understanding will deepen my spiritual practice in the Akashic Records?

25

BRIEF HISTORY

I began my journey knowing very little about the Akashic Records. There's no history book which explains, no holy manuscript to turn to, no philosophical treatise revealing secrets or techniques. Nonetheless, I spent several years researching all I could find about the Akashic Records, anything resembling them, the Akasha, the Book of Life, and every heavenly library and book reference I came across. I pieced together a timeline and assembled information on the pioneers—those who in some way figured in the history of what the Akashic Records are today. This research led me to many world religions, quantum physics, and the origins of the universe.

My study took me along a broad path of self-exploration, a path examining how people have understood themselves as human beings capable of both physical and spiritual experiences. Like the Oracle at Delphi, people everywhere across history have contemplated the message of Know Thyself. Everything associated with the Akashic Records is directly or indirectly related to this journey of self-understanding.

To create your practice within the Akashic Records, you need to know the history, the antecedents, the gifts which support your practice and provide a critical part of your foundation. Let's cover the high points to orient you *within the time and space of what the Akashic Records have been and can become.*

The first obstacle in exploring the history of the Akashic Records is that there is no definitive source with clear definitions or specific precepts explaining the hows or whys. Much of what is known today about the Akashic Records is limited by old beliefs and outdated understandings which come from association with other similar, better-documented concepts.

In a quick Internet search, the typical description is: the Akashic Records are a heavenly library containing all information past, present, and future.

While this description of a library isn't false, it is not complete.

Because there is much about divine knowing that is beyond intellectual sense and scientific proof, comparing the Akashic Records to a library is a great beginning to help understand the unknown.

However, reduced to a material object such as a library, the energetic and spiritual process of the Akashic Records is hidden, limiting both understanding and experience of the Akashic Records.

Ancient Roots of the Akashic Records

Personal knowledge is cumulative, built over time upon what is learned day after day. Yesterday's understanding combines with today's learning to create the foundation for tomorrow. Building on this foundation, what is learned today could not have been learned yesterday.

Before the printed word, knowing, the process of how we become aware, was consciously embedded in the nonlinear awareness of humanity. Our ancestors were intimately connected with the transcendent, often engaging in their lives with knowing as a spiritual practice. They lived in constant, ascended awareness of divine motion and experienced no difference between the worldly and the sacred. What remains with us today of this practice is intuition, gut feeling, and heightened awareness.

The current foundation of the Akashic Records begins in ancient, written history when the Mesopotamian ideas of divine knowing and human awareness were intimately connected with sacred, divine motion.

What is received today through the Akashic Records is both a reaching back to what was for our ancestors and motion forward into a new experience for us and future generations. It is a step beyond yesterday, a step into tomorrow.

Today's understanding brings a new focus to an ancient set of ideas. Today's learning is based on a progression of ideas. Old perceptions transform into fresh ideas and new understanding, interjected by the emergence of completely fresh awareness. Looking to yesterday's experience and allowing it to unfold in this moment offers a connection between ancient spiritual practice and the possibilities for expanding spiritual practice today and into tomorrow.

This new practice of the Akashic Records is not limited by either a specific religion or the latest self-help fad. Instead, opening to the Akashic Records today is a process allowing life to be experienced within the transcendent awareness and knowing much like our ancient ancestors.

From this transcendent view point, we can look with new eyes and find a new perspective on ancient spiritual ideas. Doing so offers a new vista to understand and experience the Akashic Records today in a future-forward perspective.

As spiritual practice, the Akashic Records connect soul journey with spiritual practice to empower individual growth and understanding.

As the soul's spiritual practice, the Akashic Records function both as bridge and transcendent connection.

Ancient Ideas Join with Modern Thought

During the 1800s and 1900s, Europe and the United States were introduced to Asian philosophy and religion. Many people began to learn about Hindusim and Buddhism due to the transmission of ideas which began during the British colonization of India in the late 1700s and early 1800s. Many new concepts and words were introduced, and translators struggled to find English word equivalents for these new philosophical and religious terms.

At the same time, there was a growing interest in spiritual matters outside the direct influence of traditional religions both in the US and Europe. Wide in scope, these interests included many esoteric areas such as paranormal activities and abilities, western magic, Hermeticism, alchemy, and Kabbalah, to name a few. This interest opened many to new possibilities for spiritual experience and understanding outside of mainstream religion.

In the mid-1850s, along with increased interest in Hinduism and Buddhism from India and other parts of Asia, a novel word moved into the English language: *Akasha*. From the Sanskrit, an ancient holy language used in both Hinduism and Buddhism, the word *Akasha* literally means to shine or radiate like the sun or stars of the sky. Defined differently within Hinduism and Buddhism, *Akasha* is generally seen as both source and container of all spiritual and physical form. The question: how to translate *Akasha* into English?

At the time, a very popular topic of both scientific research and religious discussion was the nature of Ether. As the scientific and spiritual explanation for all physical movement, including electricity, Ether was also believed to be the container of all physical and spiritual form. Viewed as similar in capacity and contents, in translation Ether was the primary chosen equivalent for *Akasha,* and the spiritual characteristics of the Ether fused with the *Akasha.*

The phrase Akashic Records, as a conduit of divine knowing, comes into the English language a little after the Sanskrit word *Akasha*, in the mid to late 1800s. Looking for an equivalency in English to further definition and understanding, the Akashic Records were also associated with the Book of Life.

The Book of Life emerged in written history from the ancient Mesopotamian concept of the Tablets of Destiny. The Mesopotamians believed that at the beginning of each year the gods gathered and determined the destiny of all creation for the coming year, recording their decisions on the Tablets of Destiny. Over the course of history, the concept of the Tablets of Destiny has been included in the Jewish Torah, Christian Bible, and Islamic Quran. In each of these sacred manuscripts the Tablets of Destiny are called the Book of Life.

In the 1800s, the recording capacity of the Book of Life was believed to happen in the Ether. Thus, the Ether as the container for the Book of Life made way for the *Akasha* to become the location of the Akashic Records and for the Akashic Records to be similar in purpose to the Book of Life.

Like the Tablets of Destiny, the Book of Life incorporates the idea that the divine knows and remembers humanity, recording lifetime deeds in a book. This aspect of divine memory is held within most world religions. Additionally, the Book of Life expressed the following thoughts about the relationship between divine source and humanity:

- God knows and remembers us.
- God has a plan for each of us.
- God values our lives.
- Evidence of God's remembrance and of God's plan is found in the Book of Life.
- Deeds in this life are recorded in the Book of Life.

- The Book of Life is used after death on Judgment Day to determine the value of life and destination in the afterlife: heaven or hell.
- The Book of Life is stored in a heavenly library.
- The recordings in the Book of Life are written by God or by a divinely designated recorder or scribe.

In associating the Akashic Records with the Book of Life, these beliefs about the Book of Life were then attributed to the Akashic Records and provide the basis for using a book in a heavenly library as the primary description for the Akashic Records. Additionally, within this association with the Book of Life, the ideas emerged about the capacity and purpose of the Akashic Records.

Though these original attributions still exist in modern thought, experience and understanding of the Akashic Records has progressed in the last 150 years. More importantly, the Akashic Records have more capacity than the Book of Life and by clinging to these now dated associations, deeper understanding of the Akashic Records is limited.

The good news is that there is a new perspective concerning the energy of the Akashic Records to which I have already introduced to you and will elaborate further upon in the next section of this book.

As you are experiencing and learning to open your Akashic Records through exercises in this book, the experience and understanding of the Akashic Records continues to progress. While the original attributions still exist in modern thought, there are incredible opportunities to more forward, to move deeper, and to move beyond. Combining historical understanding with the understanding of soul energetic dynamics (as explained in the last section) offers a path of powerful personal exploration and experience which will literally re-write history and move the Akashic Records into acceptance as an amazing source of knowing, healing, and spiritual practice.

26

DEFINITIONS FOR THE AKASHIC RECORDS

W hen I first began to teach and write about the Akashic Records, I sought to craft the perfect definition. I worked for months trying to find the right turn of phrase to describe the fullness and richness of my experience so that others would know what awaited. I wrote possibilities on strips of paper which I taped to my office wall and auditioned each clever notion that came to mind.

The short story: There is no one perfect definition. Why? Because the Akashic Records span the entire continuum of energy and, depending on experience, will be understood differently by different people.

Receiving an Akashic Records Reading doesn't require an explanation because here the primary interest is about assistance and guidance. How can the Akashic Records help me? At this point, the records are like driving the car. You don't need to understand the mechanics of the carburetor to drive to the grocery store.

However, as you begin to learn to open and connect with the Akashic Records, there is a point where some of the how and why will be very helpful in exploring the deeper roads of the Akashic Records. What you know—or think *you know—needs to be integrated with what you don't yet know for both understanding and expansion to happen.*

Let's examine several definitions to see different aspects or levels of the Akashic Records.

Definition #1: The Elevator Speech Definition

> You know that eternal part of yourself? Your soul?
> Well, as the soul makes its way through the time and space of
> the universe, it creates an energetic record.
> This record is your Akashic Record.
> It's like stepping into the origin of your soul, turning, and
> looking at your life from your soul's point of view.

This definition quickly describes the Akashic Records to someone new to the Records. This is short and simple and introduces three very important concepts.

- Presents a different perspective than the book in a heavenly library
- Brings in the concept that the Akashic Records can be understood by understanding energy
- Opens the door to thinking from the soul's perspective rather than from a body/physical point of view

Please feel free to use this definition when a new or dear friend asks, "The Akashic Records? What's that?"

Definition #2: The Bridge Definition

The Akashic Records are:

- An energetic bridge between spiritual and physical
- A dynamic archive of past, present, and future
- An infinite flow of eternal knowing
- An eternal source of healing balance
- A spiritual practice available to everyone.

Let's break this down:

An energetic bridge between spiritual and physical

Our world is now working within an integration of physical and spiritual. Able to span the spiritual and physical, the Akashic Records offer a process to initiate and experience this integration.

A dynamic archive of past, present, and future

The Akashic Records originate in the infinite and eternal and are not limited by a linear time frame. As such, access to the past, present, and future is dynamic. This dynamic access over time helps you to begin to step out of the limits of linear time and experience the multiple layers of experience that are always expanding and are accessible through this present moment, at the fulcrum of the dynamic experience of time.

An infinite flow of eternal knowing

There is no limit to the experience and expression of the Akashic Records because divine knowing is infinite and eternal. Eternal knowing offers a dance in the powerful perspective of your soul's Akashic Records.

. . .

An eternal source of healing balance

Balance is, always. Healing is balance. Awareness of balance is felt as shift and change. Opening to this awareness is facilitated by your Akashic Records.

A spiritual practice available to everyone

Anyone who believes they can learn to open their Akashic Records has the capacity to do so. Belief is followed by the need to commit to whatever path shows up for you as you learn. No one can give you belief or commitment, you must choose for yourself.

Definition #3: The Energy Definition

> Energetically the Akashic Records are a focused intention of divine knowing made accessible so that human beings may have access to the knowing available beyond physical form.

The original intention of the Akashic Records was to offer a direct conduit that supports connection and understanding between the physical and the spiritual, between the known and the unknown, within the infinite and the eternal.

Said another way: the flow of divine energy that brings forward manifested creation maintains an energetic connection which is accessible in physical form.

These three definitions build on experience and understanding. In the same way, since you now are opening your Akashic Records, you can understand that the Akashic Records are more process than a linear, three-dimensional something.

. . .

Gather what you need, open your Akashic Records, and ask these questions:

1. What are the Akashic Records?
2. How can I explain the Akashic Records to a friend?
3. What are the Akashic Records for me?
4. Within the next twelve months, what is my path in the Akashic Records?

27

STATIC AND DYNAMIC

G oosebump factory. According to one of my advanced students, when truth comes forward, the Akashic Records produce goosebumps. He always knows when he is out of his own way and clearly receiving the truth of the Akashic Records because he is all goosebumps.

I agree. Truth in the Akashic Records can be a physically received and acknowledged experience which gets your attention and literally raises the skin in reaction.

Goosebumps is what happened to me the day the Records explained the dynamic view and the static view. I had to put my pen down, look out my window, and consider what I was receiving because my body was reacting automatically, letting me know that I was receiving something significant, not to be dismissed.

The dynamic view and the static view provide key insights to understanding the current changes on the planet. What's necessary is a different view and a different trajectory of understanding. The dynamic offers this shift in perspective.

Every student I have struggles through this concept because it requires nonlinear thinking within a very linear existence. Slow, persistent perseverance will pay off.

In my offering about the Akashic Records, I have not raised the issues of grounding, centering, or forms of protection. Let me explain why.

Experience in the Akashic Records has the potential to take you beyond popular labels and explanations, to receive perceptions which go beyond the common and the expected. Open to new understanding about the world, you can step into comprehension beyond your sense of possible.

New primary concepts include the static view and the dynamic view. The static view is thinking of time and space from a linear point of view: time is simply a chronological progression of past, present, and future and space is three-dimensional, consisting of five senses.

With the dynamic view, time is eternal and space is infinite. In the dynamic view, the constraints of the linear and static do not exist. Yet, because our lives are so ingrained within the static perspective, it can be very difficult to understand the dynamic view.

One way to understand the difference is to think of static as the 1000-foot level view and dynamic as the 100,000-foot level view. In other words, the dynamic has a much broader perspective than the static, taking in much more than is possible within the static. This doesn't make what you perceive within the static wrong, simply different, and does not include the same perspective of possibility as the dynamic view.

Because the source of the dynamic view exists beyond our physical world within the infinite and the eternal, there is understanding about dynamic interpretations of reality that transcend the limitations of the static.

For example, to speak of the Records as a book in a heavenly library limits the experience of the Akashic Records to the static and the linear. There is more to the Akashic Records than a static perception. In fact, much more is *there.*

By considering the possibilities of the dynamic view, you begin to connect your awareness to possibility which transcends common linear perceptions of how the world works. This opens you to new understanding and helps create a path to that 100,000-foot view.

In this respect, the typical perspective of grounding and centering is understood only through the static view. The dynamic view offers expanding understanding. Neither is right or wrong; both offer important views.

To enter the deep road of the Akashic Records, step from the static into the dynamic. No special skill is required. Instead, release expectations and open your mind and your heart to new possibility.

Consider one of the main ideas of the static view and dynamic view— a new perception of how you can interact with and perceive time and space. Think about the process of opening the Akashic Records. The beginning of the visualization uses a process referred to as Balance between Heaven and Earth. In drawing in the energy of the Earth, you are in part grounding. In bringing in the energy of the Heavens, you are also grounding but in a different direction than Earth—which is not a common process. When the two energy flows touch and balance at your center—wherever you feel center to be—you are centering yourself within yourself and within All That Is—which, again, is not a common centering perspective. And, most importantly, the balance between Heaven and Earth is happening—whether you realize it or not—across the dynamic perspective of the infinite and the eternal and across the totality of you, spiritually and physically.

The entire opening process is creating an energy field in which you connect with the Akashic Records. This energy field contains only you and the Akashic Records held within the pure potential of the infinite and eternal and is beyond grounding and centering done within the static view.

In the dynamic view of this energy field what is important to understand is sacred space. Sacred is that which is revered, spiritual, and connected to the divine. Space in this sense is dynamic, incorporating both time and space, and the sense that it is the experience of this present moment by both you and your Akashic Records. Sacred space with the Akashic Records creates the support for this moment to be revered, held sacred, and felt as the unique, unrepeatable experience that it is. Held within dynamic awareness, there is no room for that which is not in resonance with the sacred motion of you or your Akashic Records. Thus, within the linear view protection is not necessary because within the dynamic view sacred space is naught but safe space and is inherently protective of all who enter.

Feel lifted up into a deeper experience, trusting that the process will take you where you need to go—especially if you will resist the desire to shift the process in some manner. Focus on connecting with your sense of sacred space. Focus on what resonates with your heart within the infinite and the eternal. Feel yourself supported by the divine assistance which is intrinsic to any experience of the Akashic Records. Let your troubles slide away and feel the amazing collective guidance which is the Akashic Records.

In this space, held sacred just for you, you can go beyond limitation, to see and become aware of much more than you imagined possible. The path is through the dynamic, into the depth of your heart, the expansion of your mind, the wisdom of your body, and the joy of your soul.

. . .

Gather what you need, open your Akashic Records, and ask these questions:

1. How can I understand the perspective of the dynamic view?
2. What, if any, are the benefits of the static view for me?
3. What are the possibilities of the dynamic view within current changes on our planet?
4. What else is there for me to know in this moment about the static and dynamic?

28

CHOICE AND RESPONSIBILITY

For much of my early life I had a very active critical voice inside me which liked to keep a running commentary about my faults and bad choices. Very little happened in my life that didn't come under its critical scrutiny, and the voice would quickly berate me for my stupidity and failure to be perfect. It was a voice which I tried to cover with sugar, especially the chocolate chip cookie variety. It was later the voice reflected to me by my then abusive husband. Three years into my marriage I realized that I had stopped doing anything creative because I was trying to avoid anything which could come under attack. I even reduced what I read because he and that voice didn't believe I could choose a good book.

Long story short, that realization coupled with several others helped me leave an abusive relationship before it became physically damaging. However, the emotional damage was deep and broad, and it took me years to recover. The guy was gone but not the critical voice.

In my spiritual exploration which followed the divorce and then a new marriage, I discovered that the critical voice was losing a bit of its volume, perhaps due to a lack of outside fuel. I was discerning a difference between my internal experience of myself and an external experience with the world.

More importantly, I was learning about my ability to choose in all aspects of my life. I had choice about all of me—my thoughts, feelings, and beliefs.

At this point, I learned to open my own Records and was introduced to new voices in my head and heart. One was the "voice" of my guides in my Records. The other voice was me at choice, without fear, beyond the detriment of criticism. This voice, which had been overwhelmed and dismissed, was the real me, the me empowered, balanced, and free. My voice, compatible with the voice of my Records, found strength to counter my critical voice because I realized my critical voice was powered by judgment from outside of me. My real inner voice grew in assurance and balance fueled by my personal truth. In a very emotional exchange, my Records introduced the concept of inner master and outer master. These useful concepts gave me a direct, practical perspective which, along with hundreds of affirmations also from my Records, helped me first quiet and then almost eliminate my critical voice. Gone is the slander and hurtful critique, and in its place is my real voice speaking through the balance and clarity of my inner master.

The outer master is the urge to look outside of yourself for truth and validation, to exchange your truth for another's because yours is suspect. When self-trust is challenged, then inner truth is either very quiet or hard to trust. In this place of doubt, you will feel the push to look beyond yourself to others to understand you and find your path in life. While asking for support and assistance is always a good idea, replacing your truth with someone else's truth is self-defeating. The outer master wants to create dependency, hampering self-trust and judging your truth. The outer master is not you and does not have your experience in life nor your understanding of yourself.

As self-trust builds, and inner truth begins to speak with a louder and clearer voice; you can turn from the outer master to your inner master. The inner master is the empowered voice of your true self, clearly connected to the voice of your truth. As trust builds, you build confidence in following your inner master.

Within the perspective of choice, the outer master wants to enforce what you *should* choose. A simple way to uncover the presence of the outer master is to notice the presence of "should." Thoughts of "I should do this" are often choice driven by something outside of you and not by inner clarity.

The choice of the inner master comes in the form of *must*. When you are called and are clear about a decision, the inner motion will be a declarative, "I must!" You are clear about your choice and unless you are at *must*, then whatever you are trying to choose is not worth your time. There are other versions which express *must* as "Hell, yes!" Worthy choice is powerfully declarative, aligned, and resonates with your inner sense of the absolute rightness of your choice in the moment.

In the Akashic Records, choice is important as a demonstration of responsibility. You are responsible for you, and you are responsible to make choices for yourself. Reliance on the outer master transfers your responsibility and choice to another. In contrast, your Akashic Records will encourage you to follow the voice of your inner master and to not look toward the Akashic Records as the voice of an outer master. You are always at choice and always responsible for yourself.

The Akashic Records, speaking from the origin of your soul and aware of your highest and deepest expression and intention, respond with support for you to maintain responsibility for yourself and to make choices for yourself through self-trust and inner-truth. The Akashic Records are not available to you as a replacement for your awareness. Instead, the Akashic Records are here to help you learn to trust yourself to hear your truth. No matter how much you enjoy them and they enjoy you, self-reliance is the ultimate goal. Learning to trust and hear your truth within the Records encourages you to utilize the same awareness outside of the Records in your everyday life.

. . .

Gather what you need, open your Akashic Records, and ask these questions:

1. How does choice show up in my life?
2. What stands in the way of self-responsibility and accountability for my life?
3. How can the Akashic Records help me make clearer choices about my life?
4. What is my truth today about choice and responsibility?

29

CONSISTENCY AND TIMING

D eveloping a strong connection with your Akashic Records comes from consistency and awareness of personal timing.

Consistency is not about quantity. Instead, consistency in the Akashic Records is about consistent effort over time. Focus on once every week instead of four times this week and nothing for three weeks. Chose twice a week rather than every day for eight days and then nothing for six weeks.

Life ebbs and flows, shifting, changing, unpredictable. Building connection within your Akashic Records will come out of this shift and change. The timing of your practice arises out of your awareness of what works within the changeable motion of your life.

Finding a way in which timing and consistency work together may take some trial and error. As a beginner, just learning, this is reasonable. Expecting that it magically works without effort is not reasonable. Give yourself the space needed to figure out what will work for you.

What will make a difference in your connection over the long term is simple: practice. If you don't open your Akashic Records, you don't give yourself the opportunity to learn and strengthen your connection. You miss out on what will make the difference. If you are going to do something, the only way to experience it is to simply do it. Each time you attempt to open your Akashic Records, you are giving yourself the chance of experience and tapping into an opportunity to learn.

Without practice, you miss this opportunity and eventually you will quit making attempts. In my early years of teaching, less than 20% of my students were opening their Akashic Records after one year. The difference between the students who persisted and the other 80% was simple: the 20% practiced and asked for help.

My best advice: pick one day a week, at a specific time and commit to this as your practice time in your Akashic Records. Do this every week and you will notice the difference. And then open the Records whenever else the opportunity arises.

Gather what you need, open your Akashic Records, and ask these questions:

1. What stands in my way to a consistent Akashic Records practice?
2. What can I learn about myself that would help me make stronger commitments to myself?

30

QUESTIONS

*I*n the early years of teaching, I found that many students wanted to engage with their Akashic Records but didn't know what to ask—especially questions which didn't trigger strong emotions. I created question sets and offered those to my students to help fill the gap for them.

At the same time, I heard students struggle with how to ask a question. I believe it self-defeating to judge yourself about asking the "right" question. This judgment will make trust difficult. However, it's not unusual to have something you want to ask but aren't sure how to phrase the question.

While it certainly will work to just say that you have an issue and would like to know more, there are many times you'd like to get more specific. That's where these question forms can be very helpful in creating meaningful questions for your practice.

When you open your Akashic Records, you open a connection with the presence available to you through the Akashic Records. This awareness is the Masters, Teachers and Loved Ones, or more familiarly the Guides. Sometimes you may be aware of individual entities or people, or there may be no distinct awareness of individuals.

When you open your Records, you open a direct line of communication with this presence. The Akashic Records want to be of assistance, to communicate, and to offer support. You ask questions and raise issues you want to know more about, and the Records respond within the awareness of your highest expression and the intention expressed in your questions and issues. The Records do not intend to be difficult to comprehend; they will not offer riddles or obtuse pronouncements.

When you open your Akashic Records, you begin a dialogue like a conversation with a friend. When you don't understand what is offered, you ask for clarity. If you want more information, you ask. If you want to go deeper, you ask.

To expand and deepen what is received, use these six question forms, the 5W1H Questions:

- **Who**
- **What**
- **Where**
- **When**
- **Why**
- **How**

You can use these question forms to help you create questions for your practice. Additionally, when you are in your Records, use the 5W1H forms to expand and deepen the responses you receive.

When you have an issue that you really want to investigate, use the 5W1H question forms to drill down into the topic and see the issue from different perspectives. In the beginning, students find this approach very helpful in creating questions. More experienced students will find that the 5W1H approach can help them out of a question rut.

These questions will help you clarify, expand, and deepen your understanding, creating a supportive dialogue between you and your Records.

For example:

- How does this relate to X?
- Why will X help me?
- What else can I know about X?
- When is the time to use X?
- Why is X in my life?
- Where will X take me?
- Who in my life is related to X?

Practice using 5W1H with these questions. Open your Akashic Records and ask one of these questions. Then use at least one of the 5W1H forms to ask a clarification or expansion question:

1. What is my truth today?
2. How can I open to deeper levels of trust?
3. With whom do I trust my heart?

31

CREATE YOUR PRACTICE

The remainder of this book is filled with practice for you to develop and deepen your connection with the Akashic Records. However, there is no reason not to begin to create your own questions and practice now.

I focus the questions I ask in two ways:

- What do I want to know?
- What do I want to let go?

In other words, questions are either an inquiry or a process of release, or both.

Practically, there are no limits to what you can ask, except one: questions are about you and not others. You can ask about your life purpose, but your partner's life purpose must come from his or her Records. You can ask about your relationship with others, but personal issues of others do not come from your own Records.

Avoid yes or no questions. In the beginning, receiving responses to open-ended questions is easier. Phrase your questions so that the response is more than yes or no.

Use the dialogue techniques described previously to help you develop questions. The 5W1H questions are practical, direct, and help you focus on what you want to ask.

I never fully write out my questions, preferring to jot a few words at the top of my Akashic Records journal page as reminder. However, in the beginning, you may find it helpful to write out your questions. Also remember: don't judge your questions. Trust yourself to ask what is needed in the moment.

You may also include your own questions with any practice in this book. Or you can include questions you find here with your own questions. Follow your sense of resonance with what you want to know or let go.

To help you connect with the flow, begin your practice with this question: what is my truth today? Receiving a response to this question will help quiet your mind and open you to receive, creating the space to confidently ask your own questions.

Gather what you need, open your Akashic Records, and ask your questions.

Give this a try. Think of two or three questions you want to ask.

SECTION IV

BLOCKS

Blocks on the road are to be expected.

Learning comes in the blocks as well as in the experience of the journey.

The challenge is to find the gift in the block.

No need to avoid or deny or dismiss.

Learn and receive, ready to move forward into new understanding and experience.

Each block reveals a new point of trust.

Each block reveals truth.

Trust and truth are the tools to resolve any block.

32

BLOCKS TO CONNECTION

Connection in the Akashic Records is an energetic joining where your flow aligns with the motion of the Akashic Records. Your motion has both spiritual and physical energy components, while the Akashic Records are pure potential energy emerging from and flowing through divine knowing.

Connecting with the Akashic Records is a little bit like learning how to back a car into a driveway. The driveway is a defined space like the Akashic Records. You are moving into the space in a new direction and it takes a bit to figure out how to align with the space. With practice you learn the feel of the alignment, and soon little conscious effort is required to enter.

A bit like a driveway, the process and blessing is your ritual of alignment and creates a sense of boundary with the Akashic Records as target. Repeated with each opening, both process and blessing help you develop a felt sense of alignment and connection.

Blocks in opening or connecting with the Akashic Records happen when there is a hitch in this alignment and connection process. Most often the challenge will occur within your energy. However, if you have an issue, the first step is to double-check your opening process.

- Are you including every step of the process?
- Are you saying the blessing out loud at the entryway?
- Are you going through the entryway completely?
- Are you breathing?

Review and ensure that you are completing the process in the correct order with all the components. Each step is there for a specific, energetic reason and result. Don't skip!

Because working at the soul level of the Akashic Records is spiritual practice, learning to open the Records will be deeply personal and will help you release what no longer serves you as you grow and expand. In this emerging motion, energy can get stuck. When this happens, you may feel that something isn't working right—or you may simply become aware of what is stuck. Not to worry, ask your Akashic Records for assistance. Your Records will guide release and, where necessary or beneficial, offer understanding about the source and energy of the block. Not all blocks need to be understood to be released. Additionally, some blocks may have more than one layer and require more effort to fully relinquish.

Gather what you need, open your Akashic Records, and ask your questions.

To address personal blocks, it is helpful to understand blocks in a general way. Please keep in mind that the following are general questions and not questions specific to you.

1. In general, what kinds of blocks or challenges can people have in connecting or aligning with their Akashic records?

2. For each of the blocks in the first question, ask: what can a person do to release this block?
3. Again, for each block ask: how is this block helpful for learning to align and connect with the Akashic Records?
4. Why does energy get stuck in connecting with the Akashic Records?

33

EXPECTATIONS

A common habit is to anticipate what is ahead of you on your path. If you can foresee possible events and outcomes, perhaps you can prepare yourself and avoid hurtful situations—or at least temper any trouble to manageable levels.

However, this method builds limiting expectations. Anticipation shifts your attention to what you think will happen. In the end, life usually delivers something different, and you feel caught off guard and unprepared.

Anticipation also sets up false expectations which limit awareness. When your thoughts and energy are set toward a specific possibility, you have created a limitation. If not attentive, you may miss something which could have been fantastic to receive and experience.

Some of this confusion comes from the expectations for either the journey or the destination. Destination is a determination of where you would like to go or what you would like to achieve. Journey is the experience of moving toward the destination. Nothing wrong with destination or desire or want. The trouble comes in creating expectations about the exact nature of the destination. For example, you want to learn how to open your Akashic Records—that's your destination. You think that it will be simple to learn, and because you've done other spiritual or energetic work, this should be no different. Now you've described expectations of how you will get to your destination and what the destination will look like when you have finished your journey.

For example, your journey begins, and you set out to learn to open your Records. In learning, perhaps connecting is not as easy as expected. Maybe it's easier. Maybe you are learning about yourself in a way that's unanticipated. The process of how to open the Akashic Records may be unexpected. Perhaps you thought you couldn't and find that you can. You might be having a hard time with trust. You realize opening your Records is not what you thought it would be. What you are experiencing (journey) is not what you expected (destination). Essentially, expectations differ from actual experience.

Now you have a choice to make. The conflict between where you expected to be and where you are needs resolution. Do you continue the journey? Does your destination need to shift?

Holding tightly to expectations makes shifting challenging. Inflexibility, whatever the source, will challenge you. Holding on tight to your original idea of destination may be a limitation.

Experience is bringing you new understanding and awareness in this moment. In the face of this unexpected ask, "What can I learn in this moment from the unexpected?"

Think about what you bring with you on your journey. If you bring limitation, then that's what shares your journey. If you bring excitement to explore, then your journey flows within that focus. Destination gets you going and, when you are open to possibility, the journey may move you well beyond anticipation. Journey will change you, helping you realize the essence of your destination in a way you could not anticipate before you set out. Opening to the unexpected offers opportunity to go in unimaginable directions, to experience beyond self-imposed limits.

Life is a sequence of challenge, experience, and learn which results in a sense of truth to power your next step and the next sequence. The struggle to get to truth can create its own expectation which can be hard to overcome. Perhaps you fought hard and long to get to clarity and don't expect that this clarity will be tomorrow's limitation. However, if you see yourself always open to learn, you will be able to release what no longer serves no matter its source or associated experience.

Bring yourself back to the beginning: anticipating exact outcomes doesn't help response in the moment.

Instead, trust yourself to be in this moment, willing to accept and attend to whatever shows up on your journey. Predicting outcomes and creating expectations lead you to believe that the journey is only successful if you perfectly attain the destination. Trusting yourself to respond in the moment helps release attachment to expectation. The destination shifts in response to your choice. In this energy, expectations aren't to be gotten rid of if, instead, you identify and use them as touchstones for self-discovery and learning.

Remember that as you have more practice experience in your Akashic Records you will feel more comfortable and will be less likely to create limiting expectations. Think of stepping into a creek and feeling the flow of the water. Every time you enter, the experience is different. In your Records you become familiar with the flow—the how, the content, the connection between journey and destination. Expectations don't hold you back. Instead, in trust you are empowered by the unknown of both journey and destination.

. . .

Gather what you need, open your Akashic Records, and ask your questions.

1. How do my expectations limit my experience in my Akashic Records? In my life?
2. How can I shift to understanding expectations as a source of self-discovery and learning?
3. How can I learn to let go of expectations and learn to shift my idea of destination?
4. How does my heart support my journey?
5. What can I do to release the block of expectations and improve my alignment and connection with my Akashic Records?

34

BLAME

E BFJ. Every student has some trouble with EBFJ, my shorthand for expectation, blame, fear, and judgement. Sometimes a combination of all four and sometimes one or more is predominant.

I have found that blame is particularly crippling because it will make a false filter for every experience, holding you back from a clear view. One student I thought of as the Blame Girl, because she painted everything in her Akashic Records experience with the blame brush. Most distressing was that the constant object of derision was herself. Initially, there was literally nothing I or her Records could say to loosen the hold. The puzzling part was that even though she was connected and receiving from her Records, she framed all response as proof for her blame. One day, she came to me and asked if I thought she had an issue with EBFJ. She had been reading something I'd written and related that, in the midst of reading, she felt something shift within her—like a cover being lifted—and literally a light turned on. I smiled and asked her if she was troubled. Yes, she quickly responded. Blame, the cover which has gone away.

She's no longer Blame Girl. Instead, she has developed a wonderful, loving acceptance of herself and greatly expanded her profession which had been *stifled by her blame perspective. While there is much shift and change that can be experienced in quick powerful moments, often the deepest motion takes time to release the tentacles embedded in self and can't be pushed away until the moment you just let go.*

Blame looks to the past, away from the balance of this moment. Blame tries to shift your responsibility to another source by finding fault with others, with events, or with the divine. Also, you blame yourself. Most often blame tries to defer the challenge to another time.

Facing backwards, you are out of the present moment and inattentive to the flow of your life. Blame keeps you from learning, from self-discovery, from moving forward. You can't progress facing the past. You need to be in this moment forward-facing, aware of self, and paying attention in order to choose your next step without limitation.

Blaming others is ultimately unproductive. You are the only one responsible for you. In blame, you are pushing another to assume responsibility for you. This holds you back from learning and doesn't help either person move forward. Blame keeps you from exploring and understanding at deeper levels what is being presented and how you might learn and step forward for yourself.

Blame often shows up when the unexpected appears. Blaming events is attached to the unexpected. Your hike is ruined by rain. The loud conversation by the people at the next table spoils your dinner. That's not to say that the rain and loud talk isn't happening or isn't bothersome. The choice to blame is the trouble. You always have choices about how you act and think. If you are self-responsible, then you will choose a different response in the face of the unexpected. Rain brings opportunity for different activities. Rude behavior can simply be identified as such but doesn't need to be disruptive, unless you choose that path.

Choice or the lack of choice are both fundamental. Blame is a choice you make in the face of the unexpected or the challenging. When the unexpected is unexplainable, the fallback is to blame the transcendent. Blaming God or the universe can feel like the only reasonable path when life steps into crazy and beyond rational understanding.

Life offers multiple opportunities to learn, to grow, to step beyond limitation. If you choose blame, then you turn your back on these opportunities and will miss the offered depth.

If you aren't attentive to choice, you can easily blame yourself for not being perfect, or not responding "right" in the face of the unexpected. You judge yourself and determine that your lack is the cause of the trouble. You miss that self-judgment is the block, the limitation.

When blame appears, bring yourself into the present. Ask yourself, "What is the source of my blame? Why do I make the choice of blame?"

Examining blame in the present moment helps you begin to understand what is likely to trigger blame for you. Learning about the triggers helps you make choices in the future which do not include blame. Letting go of blame, as a choice, helps you learn healthier responses in the face of life's unexpected moments.

Gather what you need, open your Akashic Records, and ask your questions.

1. How is the unexpected connected to blame for me?
2. How can I be more comfortable accepting self-responsibility?
3. Think of a time you blamed someone. What can I learn about blame from this situation?
4. Think of a time you blamed an event. What can I learn about dealing with the unexpected from this situation?

5. How can I learn to be comfortable when something I can't explain occurs?
6. What is most likely to trigger blame in me?
7. How can I release blame as a choice?

35

FEAR

There was a time in my life I would be so overcome by fear of death, I would crawl into the back of a dark closet and hide behind whatever was there. Panic induced by fear. Though I have attended to the source of the fear, the compulsion to hide was so strong I can still feel the terror which drove me, a rational being, into irrational response.

In recent years, fear has shown up for me in less dramatic ways yet still with gut wrenching, visceral motions which grab my attention and stop me in my tracks. I have witnessed the same process in my students. sometimes big sweeping motions halting them in their tracks. Other moments, fear appears in subtle motions catching one unaware.

What I have learned is that there is only one way to deal with fear: go through it. Face your fear, look for source, identify triggers, figure out what you get from the fear. Ignoring, denying, dismissing only delay the inevitable. When you look fear in the face, you will find a way through. One step at a time.

.   .   .

Fear's primal motion is worry and concern about the unknown, about what might be. Where blame is focused on the past, fear looks to the future and tries desperately to predict events yet to come. Fear dreads possibility and the anticipated damage or confusion of tomorrow, next week, next year.

Ultimately, fear is a lack of trust. The effort to predict the future is fueled by an inability to trust yourself to handle whatever, whenever. Fear pushes to solve the anticipated before arrival.

Stretched into a possible future depletes you energetically and interferes with your ability to be fully present in this moment. Stuck in the future, fear limits and blocks access to free and powerful choice in this moment.

Fear is a choice and a habit. Essentially, any effort to ignore, deny, or delay is a habitual fear response. These habits build resistance to tackling fear directly. Resistance creates illusion that fear is no longer a problem. However, instead of release, fear is building pressure within. At some point this pressure will burst, creating an emotional crisis.

Fear can also anesthetize, maiming with hollow, ineffective responses. Weakening you fuels fear to control and dominate. In control, fear will attempt to incite concern that your entire world is falling apart. However, most breakdown is not breakdown, but is instead breakthrough.

Moving in an unknown direction, breakthrough at first feels ominous because its motion is from and through the unknown. Breakthrough is neither a complete falling apart, nor is it failure. Breakthrough moves you into a new perspective with new possibility. Breakthrough moves within the unexpected and challenges you to let go of expectations and to trust yourself.

Breakthrough also reminds you that conscious, intentional response weakens and diminishes fear, making it much more difficult for fear to gain control.

The answer to fear is trust, trusting yourself that you can handle in the moment whatever appears. Trust helps you discern truth. With truth in this moment you have all that you need to claim clear awareness and conscious choice.

Please remember, getting rid of fear is not the goal. Living life to your fullest is learning to see fear as a gift. When fear shows up, don't go into resistance, don't ignore, deny, or delay. Instead, acknowledge your connection to this moment and ask, "In this moment, what is this fear offering me?" Trust yourself to receive an answer. Trust yourself to figure out your next step and the best way forward. Sure, you might still feel nervous. You might have awareness of future possibilities. But, you will also learn that you can tackle fear whenever it arises.

Whatever fear offers, transform reaction into choice, and disappointment into excited discovery. Fear is simply a reminder that you can always trust yourself.

Within your Akashic Records you find strength to interact with the unknown which expands trust and connects you with truth. Over time you will realize that you have pulled the plug on fear. You have become resilient and in trusting fully, know that fear no longer controls your life.

Gather what you need, open your Akashic Records, and ask your questions.

1. How do I allow fear to control my life?
2. What can I do to build resiliency in the face of the unexpected?

3. In what ways does the fear in politics or societal conditions affect my life?
4. What is my truth about fear?

36

DISBELIEF

As a spiritual concept, beyond religious connotations, faith is an expression of trust or confidence. When I have faith, I am acknowledging my inner sense of trust and belief.

In the same perspective, moving away from dogma, personal belief includes trust, confidence, and ... faith.

In this context, disbelief is the inability to have faith and is an indication of an inability to trust or to feel confident.

In the Akashic Records, disbelief can be directed toward the Akashic Records themselves or toward what you receive from the Akashic Records. In your learning process, disbelief may be directed at me, as your teacher, or at yourself, as the student.

As a lack of self-trust, disbelief creates a barrier as you endeavor to become comfortable and confident in opening your Akashic Records. Without trust, discerning truth is challenging and creates space for disbelief to insinuate itself and create doubt within.

Disbelief can also form when reflecting or analyzing what you receive from your Records. If everything you receive was provable, then disbelief would be easier to counter. However, the subjective truth of the records is not provable other than within you.

Some responses can be metaphorical and, if there is resonance, for you to determine. Responses outside your known, beyond expectation, also push at disbelief. Time is needed to understand the offered truth, time for you to open your heart and mind to hearing the kernels of exquisite, mystic expressions of your soul's truth.

Your mind wants to jump in and immediately analyze and determine what's right and what's wrong. The mind can get overly focused on facts as the main function of the Akashic Records. Especially in the beginning, this emphasis can open the door allowing disbelief to quickly enter.

Sometimes what you receive is an activator or catalyst for you to uncover your truth. This type of response may seem false initially and easily fosters disbelief.

However, as you settle into a consistent Akashic Records practice, your heart will begin to show up as you relax into deeper levels of trust. The energy of your Akashic Records reverberates in your heart and helps you become aware of truth resonating within all: body, mind, heart, and soul. As one of my students explains, the Akashic Records are a goose bump factory, creating a physical response in the face of truth.

With heart present, truth is easier to hear. Truth leads to trust. Trust counters disbelief. You and your Akashic Records receive your faith, disbelief is conquered, and your ability to trust yourself becomes the touchstone of your blossoming practice.

. . .

Gather what you need, open your Akashic Records, and ask your questions.

1. What is faith in the Akashic Records?
2. How does trust act as a catalyst for truth?
3. What disbeliefs do I harbor about myself?
4. What is my truth today about trust?

37

SELF-JUDGMENT

Discerning what is similar and what is different is a natural human process. Mountains are different from rivers; coffee is like water. Awareness and knowing bring forward all that is needed for discernment to occur.

However, when discernment steps into a harsher critical analysis, the process becomes judgmental and often intolerant of whatever is being evaluated.

You may walk a fine line between the support of discernment and the oppression of self-judgment. On one hand, you want to observe and reflect on yourself and your life experience. On the other hand, moving into the intolerance of critical self-judgment will only make you feel badly about yourself and will reinforce beliefs which no longer serve you in the truth of who you are being and becoming.

Self-judgment, in its harsh nature, tears down by using aspects of what appears to be truth, lobbing truth-like statements in an effort to weaken esteem and thwart self-growth. Self-judgment does not build toward the future, it pulls at the best bits within blame of your past.

The eerie voice of self-judgment exudes disappointment and failure, whispering doubt and worry. The voice of judgment tries to convince you that what is being revealed is in your best interest, if only you will admit defeat and accept the correctness of judgment.

This is a tough edge because there is always something you are working to understand and release about yourself. Yesterday's truth needs attention so that today's truth can appear and be integrated. This process requires personal discernment and loving awareness.

Stepping away from self-judgment isn't about blind or naïve choice. Honesty is required. Openness is required, as is clarity. But overly critical, harsh, intolerant assessments which tear down with only the purpose of destroying any sense of alignment or balance within self are destructive and cruel.

We all deserve loving kindness even in the face of bad choices, a lack of integrity, or cruel actions.

Your spiritual path is about trust and feeling worthy of truth. Your path is also about choice and how you choose to see yourself and live your life.

Self-judgment is a choice. You can choose to level cruelty toward yourself, or you can choose gentle support. You can choose to tear down, or you can choose the path of growth. You can choose honesty, discernment, and clarity—all supported by love. Or you can experience the path of self-hatred by speaking to yourself with harsh criticism and destructive statements.

The essence is love. How you choose judgment is an expression of love. Do you love yourself? Are you willing to find your path toward self-love? Are you open to acknowledging an aspect of self-love today that was unknown to you yesterday?

Little by little, the harsh critical voice of defeating self-judgment relinquishes control and is replaced by discerning reflection of truth.

All is possible because you are trusting yourself to be honest, supportive, and truthful about you and your heartfelt process of being and becoming. Moving away from self-judgment leads to self-love.

Gather what you need, open your Akashic Records, and ask your questions.

1. How does self-judgment show up for me?
2. What limits do I experience because of self-judgment?
3. What truth about myself is hidden behind the critical voice of self-judgment?
4. How can I learn loving discernment of myself and others?
5. How do I love myself?

38

ARROGANCE

In the *Yoga Sutras*, Patanjali speaks of *siddhi*—extraordinary or clairvoyant human skill or power. On the spiritual journey, *siddhi* act as distracting, dazzling jewels. Their shine and glitter attract attention and, at first glance, appear to be the goal of the spiritual journey. However, as dazzling as they may be, these extraordinary powers are distractions from the true objectives such as trust, truth, integrity, and vulnerability. Mistakenly, their dazzle is interpreted as worthiness and many a spiritual seeker believes that by attaining special powers, their worth will be proven.

In the presence of *siddhi*, one must be vigilant or the ego will pursue the side road of attaining *siddhi*, convincing you that this is the only worthy path. Even if you work diligently and honestly to attain a *siddhi*, your ego may delude you into believing that attainment makes you special, better, superior. The dazzling jewels yield naught but self-deception and arrogance.

Arrogance is a false sense of superiority, an evaluation of worth based on the false pretense of egotism or self-importance. The paradox of arrogance is that it emerges from feelings of unworthiness.

Distinguishing self as better than another is a vain attempt to prop up self-worth through the false belief of superiority. Often this false belief is subtle enough to distract attention from the hollowness upon which the falseness rests. For a time, you may be satisfied that you are better because of your learning or your abilities. But, at some point, the seeming superiority will be questioned and prodded for soundness and truth. The falseness will fall, unable to withstand even the gentlest of probes.

Arrogance can easily be triggered by personal issues of worthiness. Gone are the days to judge others solely to make yourself feel safer and less threatened. However, judging another to raise up the self is a subtle habit ingrained within from childhood.

The solution to arrogance is not false humility. The solution is to examine the nitty-gritty of your sense of worthiness, even though the examination may be both painful and challenging. In the peace of feeling worthy, the need for superiority does not exist.

To help you avoid the challenges of arrogance, focus on the Akashic Records as a path of learning trust and truth. As spiritual practice, the Akashic Records support your discovery about yourself, releasing whatever no longer serves. These are the activities of the spiritual journey.

Intentionally, this book does not dwell on extraordinary skill which, in some perspectives, could be viewed as the focus of the Akashic Records. Yes, you are learning a skill. Yes, opening the Akashic Records is amazing on many levels. But, it is not for the dazzle that you learn this process of knowing. Learning about the inflexible limits of your ego and the possibilities of personal growth are the honest focal points of your journey in the Akashic Records.

In your Akashic Records, arrogance can enter your efforts to feel comfortable and trusting. Ego may rear its head and push at your sense of worthiness. To connect with the Akashic Records is not simply learning a skill. Rather, this is a personal process of spiritual inquiry which requires trust. At the same time, you are building trust requiring balance, honesty, and clarity. One step at a time, just as you are, nothing to prove.

Gather what you need, open your Akashic Records, and ask your questions.

1. What do I believe is unworthy about myself?
2. Define arrogance and describe its energy flow.
3. How does arrogance show up in my life?
4. What steps can I take to release arrogance as unthoughtful reaction?
5. What can I do to find myself worthy in all aspects of my life?

39

DISHONESTY

T hough I've always thought of myself as an honest person, when I first began my exploration with the Akashic Records, I began to understand honesty and integrity on deeper levels.

My journey began with doll clothes. One day I finally saw the pile of my daughter's doll clothes stacked on the washing machine. It was a pile which had been growing for months, a pile which I studiously ignored when doing laundry, a pile of promises made and yet unfilled. I surveyed other rooms to find more stacks of unfinished projects. No single item was a huge problem, yet, taken together alluded to an issue of honesty. That evening, I sat down with needle and thread, mending what could be mended. In the next few days, I tackled the remaining piles, taking care of what I could in the moment, letting go if I knew I would not finish, or renegotiating with the relevant person for needed time.

In the process, I realized that I had a strong tendency to say yes even when I knew I didn't have time or inclination. This yes tendency was not honest, and while one yes was not harmful, a pile of unfinished yeses created a pattern that was out of integrity and not at all the foundation I wanted to create with my daughter.

. . .

Dishonesty can come with explanations and excuses — reasons for always saying *yes* that begin in childhood. As an adult, it's not a matter of excuse or judgment, simply a matter of deciding how you want to show up and how you want to treat yourself and others.

You want to be honest and truthful. You want others to believe you will be honest and truthful. This means when you say yes, you say yes because you are making a promise you intend to keep. You do not say yes to momentarily please someone.

Intellectually, you clearly understand deceit and honesty and sincerity. You understand falsehood and deception and do not want your good intentions to take you into dishonesty.

In the personal journey of the Akashic Records, you learn that as your perception of truth deepens, your awareness of personal honesty comes more clearly into focus. As trust expands, what is tolerated as truth becomes more focused. What was honest yesterday may not be honest today in the light of today's new truth.

In this perspective, judgment of self as dishonest is not truthful or necessary. Instead, accept this new awareness. To maintain integrity, be willing to accept the consequences of whatever may be out of integrity in this moment now because of new truth. Say *yes* to you, claiming the fullness of your journey with an honest and open heart.

Gather what you need, open your Akashic Records, and ask your questions.

1. In what subtle ways am I dishonest with myself?
2. How does dishonesty show up in my relationships with others?

3. Do I say yes to please others? Why?
4. How can I learn to say no?
5. What steps can I take to let go of what no longer serves me in each moment?

40

PLAYING SMALL

*I*n the first year of my Akashic Records practice, I had many doubts, *fears, and uncertainties. There was a constant push which made me step back several times and seriously question both my sanity and my truth. Maybe I'm not up to this task. Maybe I'm truly less than, missing an ability that is not mine nor will ever be me.*

I tried playing small. I tried wearing my smallness as a protective apron to the possible explosions of my ego and the dust of my less-than walk. A great deal of effort went into keeping myself downtrodden.

Thankfully, this didn't work. Why? For one good reason: playing small is not truthful.

The more I experienced my Akashic Records and the more I asked my defining question about today's truth, the more I began to feel the balance of truth within me. As my awareness of truth expanded, I began to feel the dismissive effects of playing small, of pretending to be something I am not.

I realized that playing small was its own form of denigrating arrogance aimed at dividing me from claiming the best of who I can be and become. I also saw that playing small sometimes served as excuse when connection issues in my Records arose. I could quickly blame any trouble on my unworthiness and not bother to understand the truth of my situation.

On the other end of the spectrum from arrogance is playing small. Rather than an issue of superiority, playing small is the pretense of inferiority based on a perception of unworthiness. The feeling is expressed as, "I am not good enough and am less than what is valued."

When beginning to work with the Akashic Records, it is easy to be intimidated. Working with soul energy, trusting self in this energy flow, believing in what you receive, and how you understand—all and more are often possibilities for questioning capability, understanding, and worthiness. The stakes can seem high, if not impossible. The potential for failure can be felt, just at the edges, in each moment. The push to be "right" feels unrelenting. And what is "right" in the Akashic Records? How can you reliably prove "right" beyond a shadow of a doubt?

Playing small, while perhaps motivated by a false sense of humility, is anything but humble. Playing small is defensive protection aimed at limiting pain and disappointment and will only lead to the pain of denying the truth of you.

The resolution of playing small is not a flip to the superiority of arrogance. The resolution is you and your truth in this moment— nothing more and nothing less. You!

Gather what you need, open your Akashic Records, and ask your questions.

1. How do I play small in my life?

2. What do I fear is the truth of who I am?
3. What about myself am I afraid to acknowledge or accept?
4. Is there anything about connecting with the Akashic Records which frightens or overly challenges me?
5. In this moment, what is my truth about playing small?

41

PERSONAL CONNECTION

H ow is your experience with your Akashic Records going?
Are you feeling more confident?

Are you beginning to have greater awareness of the energy flow in the Akashic Records?

Are you feeling a fluidity that wasn't there in the first few times of opening?

After a few bumps in the beginning, I was surprised to hit a big block about four months into my practice. I thought I'd gotten everything worked out. Now, I was questioning myself and doubting my experience.

At first, I was a bit miffed. But, I quickly realized it wasn't a block as much as it was a sign of improvement. I went to my Records and asked for assistance. They suggested I look directly at the blocks and seek release. Here are the questions I asked. After more than twenty years, I still occasionally ask these questions to move forward.

·   ·   ·

Gather what you need, open your Akashic Records, and ask your questions.

1. In general, what kind of blocks or challenges do I have in connecting or aligning with my Akashic records?
2. For each of the blocks in the first question: what can I do to release this block?
3. Again, for each block ask: how does this block help me align and connect with the Akashic Records?
4. What steps can I take to improve my connection with my Akashic Records?

SECTION V

CONNECTIONS

Allowing your journey fullness
Yields deep connection within all aspects: body, mind, heart and soul.

Releasing blocks offers space for connection.

No longer focused on future fear,
Connection in this moment is truth.

Connection is not perfection,
Your Akashic Records practice expands
Within personal beauty and divine power.

42

BEGINNER'S MIND

All That Is is vast, beyond comprehension, beyond awareness. Yet, on a daily basis, life makes an attempt to understand, to see, and receive the beyond.

In your urge to participate fully within All That Is, open yourself to the thrill of exploration and the joy of learning. Learn always—both the way to live and, through an invitation, to show up with your best self.

The importance of learning cannot be overstated. Learning is both the result and the method for motion, for knowing, and for intention. Essentially, life is two efforts:

I love.
I learn.

Each day, meet the circumstances of your life with love and with learning... each person, each event, each place. I love. I learn. I love. I learn.

Word. Story. Book. Library. Expressions of you and your journey in life and how you interpret and reflect on what you have learned and what you have loved.

In this context, the importance of beginner's mind is easy to grasp. When you are a beginner, you don't assume you know or that you have nothing to learn. The beginner comes ready to learn. There may be anxiety and concern about your capacity to learn, but you show up ready to make the effort.

The more you learn the more likely you are to be resistant to the new, because you no longer think of yourself as a beginner. However, each moment is expansion from the last moment. In each moment, there is something new to learn. By always being willing to learn, you are constantly approaching life with the mindset of a beginner.

Remember: the spiritual importance of beginner's mind is not a giving up of self. Rather, beginner's mind is an acknowledgment of where the best of you makes your most effective effort to engage with all of life: learning and loving.

Love, at its most essential, is full attention to ALL. When you love, you are taking in all of you and acknowledging the profound beauty of all of you: body, mind, heart, and soul. No limitations, no exceptions, no judgments. Love fully and entirely, in awe and with respect. With love, honor yourself and honor me.

In love, you learn because in love you step past boundary, obstacle, and any urge to control. Risk. Be vulnerable, eager to learn. Each moment, in love, is the beginning. Each opportunity with love is learning about yourself, about me, about the breadth and depth of All That Is.

From the tiny essence of photon to the vastness of infinite galaxies, I learn, and I love. Who you are and who you will become all emerges in love and learning. As a beginner, do not hold back, do not excuse, avoid, or evade. Show up as you, all of you, glorious and beautiful.

Learn.
Love.
Be.

Gather what you need, open your Akashic Records, and ask your questions.

1. What is love?
2. Within the Akashic Records, what is learning?
3. How can I learn about Beginner's Mind in the Akashic Records?
4. How do I hold myself back from learning?
5. In this moment, how can I love myself?
6. How do I learn always?

43

PRESENT MOMENT

This moment is the stillness between inhale and exhale.

This moment is your place of awareness.

This moment you hold powerfully in your grasp.

This moment awaits you, awaits your awareness, your understanding, your decision to be, to show up, to be present to your self's unfolding.

This moment is unique in all eternity and comes to you as infinite possibility.

This moment plays a tune for your words.

This moment is the drum awaiting the drummer. No music rings forth in this moment until you play.

This moment is hallowed as opportunity for you. In this moment you take your stand, claim your being.

This moment drinks at the fountain of eternal opportunity open for you to relieve your thirst.

Step up now from the darkness of indecision and fear. Step up now into the dynamics of this moment. Here, now, in this moment is the fullness of you, balanced with the infinite creative pulse. You in this moment, claiming connection, claiming opportunity, claiming all of you.

In this moment your awareness integrates with possibility and expands you.

Breathe in. Breathe out. Breathe into this moment.

This moment holds you at the point of discovery, of exploration.

This moment is where you begin, where you connect with all possibility, all opportunity.

Breathe in. Breathe out. Breathe in this moment.

This moment is for you.

Gather what you need, open your Akashic Records, and ask your questions.

1. What is the still point?
2. What is the dynamic view of the present moment?
3. How does breath connect me in this moment?
4. How do I find "This moment"?

44

STEPPING IN

I n a new situation, my preferred mode of operation is to circle the edges, assessing, taking note, figuring out how things are working, doing what I can to avoid embarrassment. I am, from early experience, wary and cover it up with friendliness and a sincere interest to understand other people and their desires, experiences, and fears.

As the eldest child of an eldest child, I was trained from an early age to be in charge, to watch over others before myself, to reduce burden, and avoid imposition. Travel lightly has a different meaning for me, and for most of my life I have preferred to circle and offer support from the edges.

Highly intuitive, sensitive to the energetic motion of any gathering, I also become aware quickly of possible conflict and probable connection. I have come to realize this behavior is the opposite of commitment. I am renting, not buying.

Instead of circling, I need to step in, commit, and give connection my best shot with all of me present, willing, and open.

. . .

Stepping in is commitment. Stepping in is not just a big toe in the water; stepping in is commitment to the flow of your river of life. Say a wholehearted, Yes! Give yourself a full chance with all of you present, making an effort. Dive in.

Stepping in is scary because there's no control and no guarantee. You may be mocked, or teased, or ignored. You may feel alone in the river. You may feel your river is different from other rivers in a way which will go unreconciled.

But, if you do not step in, you will never know; you will always be left guessing. If you don't step in, you will live your life in woulda, coulda, shoulda.

Stepping in gives you real data to assess your life, your behavior, and your beliefs. What works for you? What are you ready to shift? When you step in, you give yourself the opportunity to learn, grow, and expand, making it easier to step in more often. Stepping in also increases your ability to trust yourself and to trust others. When you step in, you are committing to yourself and committing yourself to a powerful process of becoming your best self.

As you learn and experience in your Akashic Records, you are giving yourself a chance to step in body, mind, heart, and soul. When you circle the records, you will find yourself caught in doubt and disbelief, limited by expectation and fear, struggling with self-judgment and blame.

Stepping in with your Records is a commitment to yourself to eliminate distance and embrace the flow of you here, now, revealing the best of you. Like all life, it is a choice, a decision, a commitment. In stepping in, you step fully into the river and you clearly claim, "The river is me!"

. . .

Gather what you need, open your Akashic Records, and ask your questions.

1. What do I receive by circling new situations?
2. What fears do I have about making commitments?
3. What beliefs do I have from childhood which make joining a group difficult?
4. How can I step fully into my Akashic Records?
5. How do I step fully into my life? What is now ready to shift?

45

PERSONAL INTENTION

L ife is a journey not a destination, yet intention and destination give direction to the journey. To set out on a journey, you need direction even if it's only a choice to wander.

The difference between direction and destination is the difference between how and what.

Destination is a what, a goal, and an objective. It's not that you won't get there or achieve or attain, the point of life's journey isn't the end.

The reward of life's journey shows up in how you journey, the experience of the direction you take, what you learn along the way.

Life isn't just about what you do, you be, you become. Life is about the process you engage in, within any given moment, and how this process is refined and adapted from experience and learning.

To begin with the end in mind helps set direction but not necessarily destination. As you live life, your intention will shift, will expand, be refined, emerging out of the truth of you in each moment.

Don't hold back trying to get to the perfect intention. Make a choice, take a step, reflect on the process, and adjust as you feel is right.

The only way to do anything, is to do it. The doing initiates a feedback system which helps you learn and refine direction. A constant process which, if you are persistent, will yield a journey beyond expectation and help you travel paths of the unknown and the unknowable.

Personal intention is not meant to be a trap. Just the opposite, personal intention is meant to not only open doors, but to create doors where needed, to expand beyond the limitation of what you think you know and support you in living your life within the infinite and eternal.

Gather what you need, open your Akashic Records, and ask your questions.

1. How do I get caught in *what?*
2. Where do I find joy in the journey of my life?
3. What will help me expand my journey?
4. What is the truth of my life's personal intention?
5. What can I do to find clarity about my life's personal intention?

46

PATIENCE

I *must confess that I have moments where I just want to yell, "Dear God,* *please, just give me the answer!" In these moments, I am done with delay* *and confusion. I am done with existing in the dark, working desperately to* *part the curtains, and see some light. In these moments, patience becomes a* *four-letter word.*

I see students with the same plea. The push and pull of life can drive you to *distraction and the deep desire to have someone provide you with answers.* *Yet the students who get beyond this push take a breath, slow down, shift* *perspective to hear with different ears and see with new eyes. Patience is* *opportunity, not delay—an opportunity not to be ignored.*

Many come to the Akashic Records for quick answers. If it's true the Akashic Records hold everything past, present, and future, then surely the desired answer can be quickly retrieved. Or, at least, that's the presumption.

However, at the soul level, the Akashic Records are about understanding and awareness, not about quick answers and responses which magically relieve frustration and delay. Response in the Akashic Records comes from a higher level and broader perception than where impatient demand usually resides.

Patience identifies that sometimes situations are out of sync or out of balance. The caution "Be patient!" urges you to take a breath and allow balance and synchronization to be found in the experience of the moment.

In contrast, impatience wants to push and pull to make balance. Impatience wants what is wanted now, beyond this synchronization of time. Impatience doesn't want to acknowledge the struggles of heart or mind. Bulldoze on through, take no prisoners, yield no line.

Impatience most often appears when trust is challenging. Impatience is felt with others as you experience troubling connection or a lack of connection. In this case, trust with someone is problematic. When impatience is with yourself, self-trust is being pushed.

A shift in perspective is always helpful when patience is challenging. To prove your value, you may push yourself to run after, chasing desire, and feeling nothing but a lack of patience with self. The more you are pushed, the further away your goal seems — impatience yielding nothing more than distance.

Rather, shift your perspective to opening and allowing, to feeling more tolerance and moderation. Instead of feeling the need to chase after, shift to receiving the flow moving toward you. Instead of running after the hard to obtain, take a deep breath and pay attention to what moves toward you.

At first, this won't be a fix-it for patience. But as you calm, you will be able to feel balance enter your experience. You will notice a greater alignment with whatever timing is presenting itself. Allow what it is you want to move toward you. The motion of allowing doesn't suck energy from you. Instead, feel support to be tolerant and accepting and...patient.

Yes, there still may be moments when your immediate desire pushes and cajoles. But now you will feel able to get ahead of the tendency toward push and counter with a deep breath and a pause. In this gap, find a thread which connects to a posture of patience and a moment to feel balance and alignment.

Trust that you will get what you want and go where you want to go. Your desire may shift and discover new possibility—all found within moments of allowing patience.

From patience, learn: Everything I need moves towards me quickly and easily.

Gather what you need, open your Akashic Records, and ask your questions.

1. What pushes me into impatience?
2. How do I not believe I will get what I want?
3. How can my connection with the Akashic Records help me find patience in my everyday life?
4. How does breath assist patience?

47

INTEGRITY

I f intention is the desire for balance, integrity is simply your internal sense of balance. Integrity is the guide for intention. Integrity is your body and soul's sense of balance or rightness with All That Is. Integrity guides the forward motion from this moment to the next present moment.

Integrity is also the internal gauge of eternal flow within. Are you aligned with your truth now? Integrity will let you know. Are you supporting the highest of your being? Integrity reveals all.

Been, being, and becoming are not individual, disconnected states; they are integrated within the energy continuum of the eternal, infinite, ineffable existence of All That Is.

Focused on your *been*, you stay stuck in fear that you are doomed to eternal repetitions of failure and disappointment.

Focused on your *being*, you over-congratulate yourself on the transformative power of your path, neglecting the solitary fact that you have lost your dynamic, sticking instead to a place of static sameness.

Focused on *becoming*, you do not let fear hold you back and you integrate transformation within a new you. Integrity shows you that becoming is never the end. Integrity guides your becoming as it transmutes into your *been*, uncovering once more new being and new becoming.

Integrity, as your guide to balance, keeps you in motion, keeps you in flow, keeps you claiming your next been-being-becoming as you transcend limit and fear with guidance from integrity.

Integrity plays itself out as trust. Can you trust yourself? Can others trust you? This is another way of saying, "In relation to yourself and others, are you in balance?" Integrity is balance. When integrity is absent, you are left with no balance and no harmony; there is a lack, something is missing.

Integrity guides your flow, signals your intention, reflects your claim. Integrity guides you to this moment within the balance of this sacred space in time, space, and spirit. Each moment requires its own response, its own sense of truth.

Let go of what does not serve, what feels untruthful within your sense of integrity, your feeling of balance. Let your integrity be your guide.

Gather what you need, open your Akashic Records, and ask your questions.

1. What throws me out of balance with myself? With Others?
2. How does balance feel within me, in my body, in my heart, and in my soul?
3. How can I know or feel imbalance?
4. How is integrity expressed within me?
5. Where do I find my integrity today?

48

VULNERABILITY

Vulnerability: leaning into the unknown without expectation.

The process of knowing can be both expansive and limiting. When knowing is focused on the known, it is very difficult to step past the content of your mind into new awareness. In contrast, focusing beyond your known into the unknown expands you on all levels body, mind, heart, and soul.

Sticking with what you know is an enticing way to manage fear. The experiences of life can build a tendency toward the path of safety and certainty. Self-protection is a natural response to the troubles and challenges of life. You want knowing to be explicit, so you can steer clear and maneuver beyond obstacles. You want answers to be able to predict which turn to make, to find the decisions which make the most sense.

However, this emphasis on knowing is fundamentally an effort to control the unknown by using the known as a source for prediction. Life is motion. In uncertainty, you desire a dependable prediction of what will happen, so you can avoid upset. Self-judgment, blame, fear, and expectations will always weigh in and find you lacking, if you can't get that "right" answer to steer clear of trouble. This push can turn you into a mouse on a wheel, running constantly but never getting anywhere.

And, for good reason: this dogged determination to get answers pulls you out of yourself where truth comes from the outer master. The paradox of knowing is that over-dependence on your known does not necessarily help you find your truth.

In the face of uncertainty, the unknown is a rich source of possibility. However, you must intentionally aim yourself in the direction of the unknown. You must step willingly into the unknown, letting go of expectations and knee-jerk reactions of I KNOW.

Essentially you need to be vulnerable, to risk safety by stepping away from the shore and directly into the flow of the river—even if you have no clue where the flow may take you.

In the beginning, stepping into the unknown can be your stiffest challenge. Every instinct within you will mobilize to keep you on the shore of your known, within the perception of safety. But, if the known had an answer, then you wouldn't be at this juncture. You come to the unknown because your knowing helps you understand where you find your truth.

You lean in, you step in, and as comfort in the unknown increases, you will dive in completely immersing yourself. Dancing with the unknown helps you see that expectation, blame, fear, and judgment are obstacles not support mechanisms. While each offers perspective to understanding, letting them control and direct your life does not guarantee safety and diverts from an inner sense of balance, alignment, and truth.

Vulnerability opens you to receive the possibility of the unknown, outside of the strictures of fear, away from limitation. Vulnerability opens the door to growth and expanded awareness by connecting you to what you don't know. Beyond limitation, you receive the unknown as ally and teacher, as mentor and friend.

Because the Akashic Records are a spiritual practice of trust, the Akashic Records help you learn vulnerability. Each time you open the Akashic Records, you are stepping into the unknown. Each opening is a receiving of the unknown through the focus of your soul. Divine knowing arises from the unknowable. It is carried by and contains the unknown. You don't come to your Akashic Records for what you know; you come for what you don't know. Trusting yourself to recognize and open to your truth, life now is experienced within the deep inner power of vulnerability.

Gather what you need, open your Akashic Records, and ask your questions.

1. What keeps me stuck in seeing only what I know?
2. How does the unknown challenge me?
3. How can I bring more vulnerability into my life?
4. What can I do in my Akashic Records practice which will help me lean into the unknown?
5. What expectations can I release to experience more vulnerability in my life?

49

EQUANIMITY

My first conscious step into equanimity came while sitting on the back step of my college dorm. I had planned on a walk to clear my head after a long Saturday of study and writing. As I stepped outside, the wind came up heavy and strong. I realized the sky was dark and somewhat green, the signs of a coming storm. Disappointed, I sat on the step trying to decide what to do. I stared into the wind and watched the trees sway, the leaves pushed into winding skyward patterns. The whole of nature seemed to breathe in, taking me into the center of its motion. I felt enveloped, held, safe within the rising of the storm. I felt beauty around me. I felt an amazing connection and, as the first raindrops began to pound the ground, I felt part of, not separated from, Earth's motion.

I don't know how long I sat, but when I finally stood up, I was soaked in more than one way. My clothes were dripping, but inside I was cleansed of my previous fatigue. My heart was light, my head clear, my body refreshed. I decided that I would never let the uncertainty or presence of weather interfere or disrupt my life. Weather in all its glory, in all its wonder, in all its unpredictability is always welcomed and will always be part of my life. I *knew that if I let "bad" weather affect my choices and my plans, I would always be controlled by something outside of myself.*

There's much in life which tries to exert control: anger, weather, disappointment, other people's behavior, dishonesty, broken electronics, out-of-stock items, beliefs, bad timing, red lights, traffic, and more. It is easy to lose composure, to get hot, to be pulled out of balance and beyond alignment.

However, your response when pushed and tested is your choice. The only person you control is you. In pressure from the unexpected, you have a choice about your response. You have a choice about how you interpret your experience.

Equanimity is calm within the storm, a choice to not be triggered into blind reaction. Rather, an opportunity to choose your action. Equanimity holds you in balance and in clear awareness. In the composure of your clarity, you can make informed decisions which further your growth and open the door to new possibility and unseen potential.

I know from personal experience that this is much easier to write about than to experience. The pressure of life ignites strong feelings and deep emotions. Everything you've worked so diligently to overcome and to move beyond can be yanked into your awareness, where there is no room to make a choice, only to react heatedly, decisively, and unconsciously.

The composure of equanimity is a target at which to aim, knowing you will sometimes miss. Missing is not a sin, not a sign of ineptitude or failure, simply a miss. Reflecting on the miss offers understanding about how to keep your composure. The criticism of self-judgment leads away from equanimity.

Let the rain pour, enjoy the showers, and step into the fullness of your life. This is not about right or wrong. Life is about your choice in this moment to support the best expression of you. Love, light, entirely you!

Gather what you need, open your Akashic Records, and ask your questions.

1. What outside factors do I allow to control my life?
2. What can I do to release these factors?
3. How can equanimity show up for me in my life?
4. What holds me back from experiencing equanimity?

50

WORTHINESS

*A*m I good enough?

Am I worthy?

Am I inherently of value?

Life is priceless, invaluable. In the face of this divine undefinable which surrounds me, how do I measure up?

How do I calculate my worth, my value, and if it exists, my own pricelessness?

Everything about you is wrapped up in your valuation of yourself. Everything. Every issue or obstacle somehow, someway relates to your sense of self-worth. Every action, every decision, every moment is filtered through your lens of self-worth.

Why? Because every person on the planet questions his or her value. Every person feels compelled to prove their value. Every person feels that their value is in question from the day they are born until the day they die.

From the beginning of written history, story and myth revolved around worthiness. The day of final judgment is entirely about ascertaining worth. Karma is an assessment of value, worth, and failure. Divine rewards recognize merit and worthiness. Life experience is an unceasing push to prove worth and value.

The idea of being in service is also a worthiness issue. If you help others, perhaps you can do enough to prove your worth. If the one you help is suffering dire circumstances, you will hope to attain even more credit and value.

Yet, no matter what you do and how much you serve, you are left questioning, left wondering, "Am I good enough?" You set out again, reaching out, grabbing whatever outside of yourself may help prove, beyond anyone's doubt, that you are good enough.

However, there is nothing outside of you that will prove your worth. Worthiness is an inner, personal experience. No matter what you do, you will never be able to satisfactorily prove your value.

Why? Because your value is intrinsic. Your value doesn't require proof to exist. Your value is inherent and has been part of you from the original moment of your soul's awareness. Your value exists as part of you. It cannot be and doesn't need to be proven.

Seeking personal value by looking outside, will lead in the wrong direction. Looking inside, you find your worth, quietly hoping you will notice and stop your futile search.

Your worth is a beautiful melody of balance and alignment able to shift rhythm and tune as you experience life, make choice, and trust yourself in your truth.

Not about right, enough, or perfect.

Open. Allow. Accept.

Always, you are worthy.

Gather what you need, open your Akashic Records, and ask your questions.

1. What makes me feel not good enough?
2. How does my value for perfection create inner obstacles and misunderstandings?
3. How can I break my habit of looking outside of myself for validation?
4. How does self-trust support my acceptance of my self-worth?
5. What is my truth today about my self-worth?

51

BALANCE

One of the more perplexing concepts I've explored in the Akashic Records is this:

Balance is.

My first thought was that my Records were being a bit too subtle. Occasionally my guides offer little bits for me to assemble toward a path of deeper meaning. But, two words? I consciously stepped into beginner's mind, trying to open the door pass my rigidity. I asked, "What does this mean?"

Their response, "Balance Is and does not need to be created."

Balance exists and is not something I need to make or find or create. An interesting idea yet contrary to how I've always thought of balance. Balance feels like an experience of shifting weight until the two sides of the scales are even. Seen this way, balance is up to me to create. However, as I thought and struggled, I began to understand.

Balance Is—a different perspective, one which pushes at what I think I know.

Balance Is—the unknown sneaking into my awareness, asking me to release expectations and move beyond into uncharted territory.

Balance Is—brings to me all the possibilities of perception contained within patience, vulnerability, equanimity, and worthiness.

Balance Is—a perspective helping me to rise beyond limitation, fear, and expectation. A perspective that is exactly what I want for myself, I will not let this opportunity pass me by.

I asked, "Why isn't balance created?"

Their response, "Because the thought that balance needs to be created is a static view limitation. Balance Is—this is the gift of a dynamic view."

Balance Is—insight from the dynamic view. This was an A-Ha moment for me.

The floodgates opened, a powerful uplifting flow, introducing me to vision beyond my expectations and limitations.

In each moment, Balance Is.

In each moment, you learn and expand, truth shifting within you. Balance dynamically shifts with you, in alignment with your truth. Feeling out of balance is simply a feeling and not an actuality. Instead, feeling a lack of balance is not knowing where, in this moment, Balance Is. As truth shifts, balance shifts. Balance Is always, but not always in the same place.

Fear, expectation, blame, and judgment—all make clear awareness in the moment challenging. However, understand the motion of each to find awareness and feel into where, in your life ,Balance Is.

In the same way, patience, vulnerability, trust, and equanimity support clear awareness. For you and from you, each are products of Balance Is.

Life is not a choice between two oppositions. Rather the oppositions, perceived from the dynamic view are unified into the motion of spiritual and physical integration.

Balance Is, with your body, your mind, your heart, and your soul.

Feel into balance, allowing the unknown to bring awareness forward and support you in this moment.

This breath in. Balance Is.

This breath out. Balance Is.

Gather what you need, open your Akashic Records, and ask your questions.

1. How do I push against feeling balance?
2. What triggers me into feeling out of balance?
3. What fear gets in the way of my awareness of balance?
4. How does Balance Is assist my connection with the Akashic Records?
5. Help me feel balance in this moment, so I can feel balance in any moment.

52

HEALING

To mend. To make better. To restore. To make new. To release. To find balance.

The most powerful healing comes in openness to release, to shift, to accepting a new perspective within responsibility for yourself.

Healing is a process for the self, by the self. You heal you.

A healer holds space to mend, to restore, to find balance. Claim you as healer for you.

The healer offers unexpected attention to that which needs awareness of balance. In your openness to this view, you release, finding balance in the unexpected within you. Attention to the unseen, or the denied, brings forward a new view which releases blocks and removes obstacles. This is particularly true with trauma. As frozen energy, trauma needs a softening and a melting to restore the energy motion along the continuum.

The energetic motion of healing gains momentum in the asking of support. In the Akashic Records, healing is both subtle and obvious.

The key is to seek balance and to move beyond expectations. The origin is beyond belief and expectation. Allow your Records to guide you to awareness were shift and release happen without demand. Healing cannot be pushed or cajoled. Healing moves toward you, along the path of least resistance, in response to your highest expression.

Look to your breath, to your knowing, to intention. Think on cleansing or claiming. All will be involved in your process of healing.

Don't assume, instead, ask. Explore possibility to move beyond expectation and limitation.

Healing removes barriers and can feel like breakdown. Instead, healing is breakthrough.

Healing is not always happy endings because highest expression isn't about compromise or neglect of truth. Truth does not defer truth. Truth simply is, even if you don't like or want "that" truth.

Balance doesn't always rest in the place of your liking. A block released reveals the light of the healing you have received. Acceptance reveals the balance offered by your healing moment.

Breathe in. Feel into your heart and recognize balance. You have accepted healing for you.

Gather what you need, open your Akashic Records, and ask your questions.

1. How can I offer the sacred space of the healer to myself?
2. How can I experience healing in the Akashic Records?
3. What message do you have for me about healing as balance?
4. How is motion involved with healing?
5. How is knowing involved with healing?

53

SACRED SPACE

As this breath inhales, there is a moment of stillness before you release your breath in exhale.

This moment is of peace and the silent wonder of joy, as possibility steps forward to guide.

This is the essence of sacred space. Your burden is released, your environment is purified, and you are fully present to all of your being in this moment.

Here intention unfolds within the agreements of your integrity. Here your flexibility allows you to stand in witness to your own unfolding. In sacred space, judgment melts away as you stand within yourself with truth as your guide.

Sacred space is cleaning away the debris of your connection to All That Is as you feel within the wonder of infinite possibility.

Sacred space is unending, unguarded, unblocked flow of infinite connection as she allows you to hear and feel and understand in this moment your truth, your goodness, your ability to love.

Let this moment swell in your heart. Let this moment solidify your joyous understanding.

You can feel the possibility; you can sense the potential.

Sacred space becomes sacred vision felt within as its picture blossoms from your heart, from your connection with All That Is.

Sacred space warms the soul and calms the mind as you find the still point within.

This breath in. Release.

This breath out, release.

Let go of all that does not serve; set aside, for a moment, all which is not to be finished.

You, in this moment of Sacred Space.

Gather what you need, open your Akashic Records, and ask your questions.

1. What are my elements of sacred space?
2. What can I do to prepare myself to step into sacred space when I open my Akashic Records?
3. What can I do to live within sacred space in my everyday life?
4. Show me my personal feeling of peace within sacred space.
5. What steps can I take to move into sacred space at any moment?
6. Is there anything else that the Akashic Records would like to tell me about sacred space?

SECTION VI

DEEPER ROAD

The Deeper Road comes when your creative being soaks in the
unknown and the unknowable.

Vulnerable, open, willing to risk all,
The Deeper Road becomes your path,
The source of your journey.

Heart open, soul afire,
Journey and life joyfully inseparable.

Trust and truth fully claimed.

You have entered your Deeper Road.

54

MEMORY

Welcome to this dance we call life: a waltz, a tango, a polka, the two-step, the swing. Misstep here, slide and twirl there, turning forever into the next step, the next dance, in this life. Dancing alone, with a partner, following, leading... meld to a music beating within, pumping you with passion and joy. On you go creating the dance, its steps, your response, your lead, your follow.

Memory powers your dance, bringing you the next step seemingly from nowhere. In the beginning as you learn, you must think through each step, each movement here and there. As the steps begin to flow, your attention moves to your partner, to the music, to the other dancers while memory, now unconsciously recollected, keeps you upright, in step, with the beat, smiling, enjoying this moment in flow with the dance.

Observer and observed, lead and follow, spinning within the eternal and the infinite, changing places within the fluid dynamics of life until there is no sense of you and me, only the dance, the one, knowing and memory pulsing as one.

In the dance, memory can be of image and of bodily sensation, of thought and feeling, of love given and received. You witness your dance and the dance of others. Each step driven by joy to take another step as memory provides the bridge between the last steps and the next steps.

You observe and are observed, observation integrating with feeling and thought, creating new movement, new feeling, new thought, a new dance to experience within and without.

Where does one start; where does one end?

In the dance you learn in love by heart.

Gather what you need, open your Akashic Records, and ask your questions.

1. How can I expand my sense of time in my everyday life? Give me an image which represents this expansion.
2. How can I shift my awareness of memory into a dynamic view?
3. How does my yet unknown future impact this present moment?
4. How does my body awareness connect with thought and feeling to help me be aware of my authentic being?
5. How do I become aware of the dynamic recording of my life in this moment?
6. How can this awareness help me understand my highest expression?

55

UNDERSTANDING

Judgment is easy, while seeking to understand takes time. It is always easier to immediately judge the mother yelling at her child or the thief caught with stolen goods in hand. Judgment comes rolling out of your head and down your tongue without a moment's consideration. Judgment makes you feel safe. You feel judgment puts you in control.

Understanding takes practice. Understanding others requires that your first thought is as *We*. Understanding requires that you take a breath, hold still for just a moment in the presence of the mother and the thief.

In this moment, perhaps on the intake of one more breath, you stop judgment in its easy tracks. In this moment, you choose a different path, you take another breath, you hold still a moment longer while you consider, while you reach out and place yourself in the other's shoes. In this moment, you can come up with a million reasons why. In this moment you become the mother, the thief, the enemy, and they are no longer separated from *Us* as *Them*. In this moment you know that you can begin to understand. Judgment ceases and the possibility of love steps forward. *Us and Them* fold into *we*. We are We.

The willingness to release judgment and to embrace understanding is a primary requirement to work in the Akashic Records. In judgment, your known remains static, held hostage to the belief that you already know everything. Judgment creates a wall around your limited known, choking off any access to the depth of divine knowing.

In the Akashic Records, understanding comes by acknowledging you do not and cannot know all. Instead of quickly making up your mind, you observe, allowing your truth of a situation or a person to be revealed within the quiet of your witness.

Judgment feels compelled to holler its dismay and disapproval. When the decisions you make are tempered by love and the willingness to let truth emerge, then understanding unites, bridging the lonely, the hated, the misfit with tolerance, compassion, and loving comprehension.

The Akashic Records are here to support you on this journey within WE not as judge but as witness to the love of understanding.

Gather what you need, open your Akashic Records, and ask your questions.

1. What can I do to improve my ability to witness myself and others?
2. What about my judgment keeps me from viewing the world with a dynamic focus?
3. How does judgment separate me from others?
4. What can I shift within myself to open my judgment to possibility?
5. What shift within me will help me see beyond my known?
6. At what point do I experience an inflexible sense of myself?

56

DESTINY

Choices are the hinges of destiny. When you turn your attention to Now, to the present, you find the fulcrum between the fate of necessity and the allotment of destiny exists as choice. You are endowed with the power of choice, even if your only choice is to believe you are not bound by a pre-determined fate.

Your focus moves from the past to the present allowing destiny to step up. Your imagination can take flight, your reason can inform decisions, your heart can follow deep intention. You can choose to be the master of your destiny. You commit to yourself in your freedom of choice. Your life is no longer about the determinism of cause and effect. Now you face the future focused on your path, your dreams, and your desires.

When you make a choice for yourself, you risk: the outcome may not be what you thought you wanted. You determine your life. Face to the future, you stay focused on this moment of interweaving who you are with the possibility of who you can become. You willingly take the risk not because choice gives you control, but because through choice you find the path into the fullest possibility of who you are in the universe. You turn. You choose. You risk. You live.

Destiny is not just the course of your life and the fortune or misfortune you encounter. Your life is more than the fates chronicled in your individual tablets. Destiny springs from your own personal characteristics, who you are, your natural gifts, your abilities and talents, your intentions for this life. In your unique possibility you find choice, that ability to make the determinations of your life your own.

Fulfillment of destiny becomes your ability to rise from the present and unfold your divine endowment, to find yourself, your path, and to explore and create your divine legacy for yourself. Destiny ascends from the present to allow you to claim possibility and fulfillment as divine providence. You make the ultimate choice: together, you with the eternal write your own tables of destiny. In choice, you find connection with the unknowable. In the now you understand. Destiny is your claiming of the divinity within.

When you think of the Akashic Records as an actual book containing the history of your life, you unwittingly limit yourself to static fact and imposed fate. From an energetic point of view, the Book of Life exists within the continuum of energy as an eternal flow of your potential into form. In this perspective, the Akashic Records, no longer confined to the superficiality of the printed page, expand into the flow of choice and possibility, into the flow of being and becoming. The Akashic Records are of destiny where you find the choice to live your life powerfully in this moment where all is good, and the future is open—to you!

Gather what you need, open your Akashic Records, and ask your questions.

1. What habits, beliefs, or stories no longer serve me?
2. How can I observe the flow of All That Is in my everyday life?
3. How do I allow myself to open to infinite possibility?
4. How do I narrow my choice? What can I do to expand choice?
5. What effect will this have on the integration of spiritual and physical in my life?

57

CREATIVE BEING

You are created from the material of spirit and the spirit of matter, animated by the awareness of Universal Life Force, the force by which potential becomes form.

Integrating the potential of the spiritual with the potential of the physical, human form is created as a facet of awareness of All That Is.

You are the knowing of All in form. You live in a creative world. All you know and imagine is creation. The fundamental nature of the universe is one of creative endeavor: originating the possibility of the unknown, bringing forward the new, constructing your imagination, building your dreams. This occurs because All That Is is creative awareness, an awareness that stimulates potential to take form.

Within this creative awareness of All That Is flows the energy from which you emerge. Moving always along the energy continuum from potential to form to potential, energy is creation. In this perspective, creation is infinite and eternal, always moving and responding to the inner intention of its energetic impulse. Through its awareness of All That Is, creation beholds all possibility and responds in an eternal dance through the infinity of all to bring forward the form of potential.

Creation is not a solitary experience. Rather, creation moves within and between all the facets of individual potential and the integrated, inter-connected, collective experience of All That Is. Try as you might to force creation to be a lone force, on the contrary, creation is always co-creation, an experience between all soul points and All That Is. Creation is a mutual realization of the possibility of your potential as form.

Gather what you need, open your Akashic Records, and ask your questions.

1. What is my intention for participating in life? How can I become clearer about this intention?
2. What gets in the way of deep and clear breath?
3. How am I a creative being?
4. As co-creator, what is my next step in participating in All That Is?

58

CREATIVE WORD

Word is divine sound made manifest. The original creative sound lives on within the words of language. You continue to respond to the creative intention embodied within the word in whatever form you encounter. Whether you meditate on the first utterance of the divine, devote time to the chanting of mantra or the singing of prayer, or contemplate the story contained in the latest novel, you are called to the same action every time you encounter the word: you must find meaning.

In whatever manner it is expressed, the basic intention of any word is to call into creation an opportunity to find self, to find truth, to find divine sound in life.

As sound, the word creates connection, a bridge between the unknowable, the unknown and the known. You feel, you think, you respond, answering the call to creation. Crossing this bridge is opportunity for understanding, expanding knowing, expanding possibility, expanding your own sound, your own word. Word ignites meaning for your discovery.

In this perspective, the Akashic Records is the sounding of the Word. When you come prepared to accept responsibility for the focus and direction of your life, entering the Akashic Records is a request to hear Your Word, to initiate the creative flow of energy which lifts you, supports you, and gives you room to fly.

Hear Your Word. Sound Your Word. Live Your Word. Whether flowing across your lips or across your page, Your Word flows from your center toward intention. Word ignites potential, creating your highest expression of form.

Your Word, created by you, creates You.

Gather what you need, open your Akashic Records, and ask your questions.

1. What word or sound can I say to open my awareness to the motion of my soul?
2. What is my soul's word?
3. What is the divine's word within me?
4. How am I divine sound made manifest?

59

CREATIVE ACTION

To experience your soul's urge to participate, you embrace your role as creator. Your intention continually leads you to experience over and again the flow of potential to form within the dance of All That Is. Intention to take form brings you into Physical Reality; your urge to unite with All That Is encourages you to express your infinite potential within, over and over.

Creativity naturally wells up within as you seek to participate. The creative expression need not be grand gestures or famous actions. The deceptively simple act of breathing in and out is the ultimate creative action. Every moment of your life you are experiencing and expressing your creativity.

During this creative process, you bring the energy of All That Is into yourself through your Divine and Earth Connections. Three energy flows (physical, spiritual and universal) intermingle to bring form to the potential of your urge to create. The mix of energies creates form, but the mix also creates new universal energy within you which flows back through your Divine Connection, adding new potential energy to All That Is. Your creative impulses expand the universe. Your form creates new energy, and without the resistance of your physical reality this creative process would not be possible.

The creative expressions of both Non-Physical Reality and Physical Reality are dependent on each other. Potential from Non-Physical Reality takes form only in Physical Reality while the form of Physical Reality creates new potential for Non-Physical Reality.

Neither physical nor spiritual are better than the other; physical and spiritual are mutually dependent and mutually necessary to provide the opportunity and the floor for your soul's eternal, creative dance as potential to form to potential within the eternal wonder of All That is.

Gather what you need, open your Akashic Records, and ask your questions.

1. What beliefs do I hold that interfere with my creative expression?
2. How could I re-create myself to feel balance within?
3. How can I create my life within the balance and integration of the physical and the spiritual?
4. What message about me, as creative being, do my Masters, Teachers, and Loved Ones have for me today?

60

DEFINING PURPOSE

Why are you here, now, living the life you are living?

How can you evaluate the benefit or value of your life?

Are you doing the "right thing" in your life?

What is the "right thing"?

The usual definition of one's purpose is the reason you are here and what gives your life meaning and worthiness. If you understand your purpose, then you have a foundation to answer these questions.

However, purpose as reason and meaning is a static view where purpose becomes a standard against which the value of your life is measured and validated. This leads to a constant journey out of self to define and find you. Thus, *defining purpose*, in the static view, is an outside-focused effort to value self. It's a rat race, a never-ending run after something that doesn't exist, because purpose is not a thing you find.

Instead, think of *defining purpose* in a dynamic sense. To define means to seek understanding, clarify parameters, and dynamically seek in this moment. Expansion from moment to moment, within the process of creation, allows a new definition in each moment of asking.

Purpose, in the dynamic sense, provides a focal point for the present moment which moves you with little resistance into the next moment. Seen this way, purpose is about resonance in the moment. You are not going after something outside of yourself, instead, you are focused within the balance and alignment of who you are and can become in this moment. There is not one purpose forever; there is a focal resonance for each and every moment of your life.

To truly define purpose, shift away from the static approach. Shift your perspective into a dynamic awareness of this moment. Incorporate all that you are learning, especially about the present moment, resonance, creative action, and dynamic view, to liberate and define purpose in this moment.

Approach *defining purpose* as inner, personal process attended to in this moment.

Think of *defining purpose* as calling, as the voice of you speaking your truth in this moment.

Incorporate *defining purpose* into the flow of your life and allow it to bring guidance and support from the depth of you connected always to divine knowing.

Gather what you need, open your Akashic Records, and ask your questions.

1. What within me needs releasing to incorporate creative action within the present moment?
2. How do I align with resonance to claim the dynamic process of *defining purpose*?

3. What steps can I take to incorporate the dynamic process of *defining purpose* into my everyday life?

4. Choose an issue or topic in your life in which you would like to define purpose. Ask: Within this issue/topic, how do I dynamically define my purpose which supports my being and becoming in this moment?

61

LEARNING

Focused in the static view, the process of learning overly emphasizes acquiring knowledge as facts or information. Information is needed to live life but is not the only way to interact with knowledge. The dynamic view of learning opens awareness to knowing as a process in which resonance, balance, and alignment are both guide and platform for expansion within the moment.

To learn, first you must open yourself to the fullness of possibility. As you learn, you will also release learning from yesterday because, in view of the new, the outdated is no longer relevant or useful. This release process can be challenging especially when learning is hard-won or was life-changing in the moment. However, accepting the process of *defining purpose* as dynamic experience, opens the door to experience learning in the same way. Learning dynamically reinforces the awareness of purpose in the moment. Together, you have a way to support yourself as you engage the entirety of your life within the perspective of dynamic awareness.

Learning is then expressed in each and every moment of your life. You resonate on all levels with this dictum: Learn Always. While you may always focus learning towards specific experiences or topics, learning in each moment is you and how you engage with your life.

Learning is the openness to consider new perspectives, letting go of expectations and what you think you know. Learning is done through awareness of your worth and your ability to assess and align with that awareness in each moment. Learning doesn't tear you down in a negative or destructive way. Learning builds you, enlarging your worldview, supporting the release of the no-longer needed. Learning is intrinsic to your path because you trust yourself to receive your truth. Fully integrated with your inherent process of being and becoming, learning nurtures and supports the power and strength of your essential core in balance with All That Is.

Your life, in this moment: Learn Always.

Gather what you need, open your Akashic Records, and ask your questions.

1. What are my personal, static notions about learning?
2. How do I release these notions?
3. What can I do to release trust issues I have about learning?
4. How does the dynamic approach to learning support and enhance my self-worth?
5. How can I embrace learning as a dynamic process in my everyday life?
6. What is my truth today about learning?

62

LOVE

L ove is the ability to take in the beautiful completeness of an individual. Love holds no judgement; it accepts the awareness of faults and challenges as part of the human experience. Love is the experience of heart connection within balance, alignment, and resonance.

There are different kinds of love — yet love at its essential core is connection and awareness of the connection. Connection provides a conduit for energy to flow. Love is energetic exchange through heart to heart connection. Love creates a shared energy field which holds both in awareness of the possibilities and experience of the deeper road. Not all walk this road, but when trust, truth, and learning are conscious experiences within the connection, love is the energetic resonating experience shared by those so connected.

Love comes through the heart. Love sings in the soul. Love is the experience when heart opens to the flow of connection and exchange.

In this moment, bring your attention to your mind and feel connection. Bring your attention to your body and feel connection.

Now, bring attention to your heart and feel connection. Feel your body, mind, and heart connect and exchange loving energy.

Love begins with you, within you, as foundation and as connection with All That Is. This connection of love underlies all connection with each person in your life and with all people throughout the world. Love is not a randomly-chosen expression. Instead, love is part of all of you, all your being and becoming, all connection with all experience.

Love is, always. By being alive, you love. By being aware, you love. By experiencing life, you love. Love is your choice within your awareness.

A closed heart limits and can eliminate awareness of love within your life. An open heart experiences and encourages awareness of love. An open heart learns always about love, in this moment, and resonates with the awareness of the connection of love—not expecting, but acknowledging what is, in the moment.

Because love establishes connection, this opens the heart to pain. What flows in this connection is not always experienced as joy or pleasure. Sometimes heart connections jerk at the heart, wounding the flow. Why does this happen? Because that is the nature of Love. Love does not resist flow, nor does love judge or condemn. Love, by its very nature, is open to all flows of energy. In the dynamic view, there is neither bad nor good, but connection and experience of the flow between hearts open to the essential fullness of life. Pain felt in the heart is learning experienced at the deepest and most profound levels. Love can't be chosen only to feel good. Love is an expression of All That Is within the unique facet that is each being. To be open to love is to open the heart to all flow without judgment. Learning helps you process the experience and remain open when love becomes uncomfortable or painful.

Love is a challenge to engage with your life with open mind, body, heart, and soul. Love asks you to show up fully, aware of connection, and open to learn. In your openness, you will be able to experience, process, and learn about the individual nature of love for you, from youself. Exchange and connection mean love filters through you and becomes an expression of you. The pain of love comes when your expression does not resonate within the offered expression. The joy of love is a full experience of shared resonance within the energy exchange and connection.

Just as you are learning always, you love always. The fundamental expression of all humanity is love. Love exists even when awareness is absent. Learning about life brings awareness and, within learning, love comes more easily and with less trouble.

Trust is a form of love. Truth is an expression of love. You are always worthy of love.

This is your life always: Be yourself always. Learn always. Love always.

Gather what you need, open your Akashic Records, and ask your questions.

1. How can I open my mind to experience love?
2. How can I open my body to experience love?
3. How can I open my heart to experience love?
4. What stories, beliefs or thoughts about myself do I have that interfere with my ability to receive and offer love?
5. How do I experience love and open my heart to connection in the experience of love?
6. How do I love myself? How can I expand my self-love?
7. What is my truth today about love?

63

SOUL PURPOSE

E nergetically your soul is an experience of individual awareness, held within the flow of the infinite and the eternal.

Dynamically, soul is not material manifestation. Rather, soul is experience or expression of a unique facet of All That Is. As a process, soul enjoys interaction and exchange much like a feedback loop experienced across the infinite and eternal.

Think about this: **soul is experience across the infinite and the eternal**.

This means, for you, that your soul is motion, is intention, is knowing. Your soul is energetic experience.

Let this sink in deeply, fully. When it does, your life will change, shift, and move in a new direction.

———

Purpose as experience is not solitary, or fixed, or predetermined. Purpose as experience is expression in the moment and awareness that emerges with the expression. Purpose as experience utilizes the entirety of you to make known truth in this moment.

When you set out to understand your soul's purpose, you are actually setting out to find the deepest energetic expression of you in this moment. You may mistakenly believe that your quest is to be told in static words, a definition, an explanation of your soul.

However, dynamically seeking soul purpose is a vision quest of the most profound, powerful expression of you within the depth and breadth of the infinite and the eternal. This quest is a journey to understand the essential core of you as body, mind, heart, and soul. This quest is supported by trust and truth, by learning and love, by your willingness to be vulnerable and release expectations, judgments, and fears born from the limitations of a worldview bound by linear blinders.

Instead, step forward into this moment and truly hear your soul calling to you. Feel yourself connected to the depth and breadth of infinite possibility. Open yourself to experience, to connection, to awe.

In each moment, your experience is your soul purpose - an experience to help you move beyond boundary and limitation.

Trust yourself to touch your depths. Learn to live from this depth. Love yourself within the peace and beauty of you.

In the first moment of soul awareness, the divine saw all of you, all your potential to be and become across the entirety of the infinite and eternal. This was your first experience of love, of divine love. In this moment, you are also seen by All That Is as the magnificent being you are, now manifest within the beauty of the world. Your soul is origin. Your soul both births and is birthed by the creative action of All That Is. In this creative dance, you learn love.

. . .

This is your soul purpose: Live your soul as experience of divine love.

Live. Learn. Love. Now.

Gather what you need, open your Akashic Records, and ask your questions.

1. What expectations, judgments, and fears limit my worldview and my understanding of soul as experience?
2. What blocks me from claiming my soul as experience?
3. What may I do to experience soul as intention, motion, and knowing?
4. What is the deepest energetic expression of me in this moment?
5. What is my truth today about my soul purpose?

64

LIFE PURPOSE

Like soul purpose, life purpose is an incredible expression of the depth and breadth of you as a manifested being. This is not about finding words or seeking answers outside of yourself . Instead, life purpose is a journey into the depth and power of who you are and are always becoming.

To explore your life purpose, you need two abilities: learning and loving. The good news is that, as a human being, you inherently possess both abilities. The work comes in making sure that you practice both on a daily basis and each moment of your life. No exceptions.

Passion comes in the intersection between the depth of your learning and the breadth of your love. Passion is expression of resonance within your body, mind, heart, and soul. Very simply, life purpose is an expression of your passion.

As a soul of infinite capacity, there is no limit to what you can do in your life, and there is no one requirement to fulfill. The earth is making titanic shifts away from physical domination toward life lived within physical-spiritual integration. In this universal motion, the purpose of your life will shift and shift and shift as you learn and love and engage with your life as a dance of joy and exploration.

Life purpose is not one thing. Life purpose is the one thing you are passionate about in this moment. What do you love? What brings you joy to experience in this moment?

Here's the question: Knowing you cannot fail, what will you do with your life?

The only block in the way of living life purpose as passion is failure. You want to succeed, you want to do what you want to do, yet at the same time, you do not want to fail. There is pain and disappointment in failure. There is embarrassment because failure seems to indicate that you are less than, incapable, broken and unrepairable.

However, the only failure that matters is not making the effort to live your life through your passion. Deciding to compromise the best you are for the safety of possibly not failing is the worst failure. That's deciding you are not worthy of your best. That's not trusting yourself at the most fundamental level. That's turning your back on learning and loving.

The only way to live the depth of the experience of you is to look failure and all its associated fears in the eye and say no. Claim your life through passion not through fear. Now, you can follow your heart and express the best of you. The purpose of life is to learn and love. The purpose is to not let fear and failure dictate.

With passion as your guide, you can create your life based on your awareness of resonance, alignment, and connection. You don't need to look outside for clues. Instead you look within, trusting yourself to receive your truth, to connect with the flow of your learning, and to follow the lead of your heart open to love.

Dynamically connected, life has purpose because you learn, and you love. Passion is your guide, moving always beyond failure and fear.

Let passion be your purpose and guide within a life lived with trust and truth in each step.

Gather what you need, open your Akashic Records, and ask your questions.

1. How does fear of failure block my life?
2. How can I release fear in the moment it appears in my life?
3. What inhibits me from recognizing and living my passion?
4. What can I release from my heart which no longer serves me?
5. How can I harness passion to support my being and becoming?
6. What brings me joy to do and experience in this moment?
7. What is my truth today about life purpose?

65

FINDING THE DEEP ROAD

P laying small is also playing safe. Granted, the compulsion for safety often stems from pain; safety is an illusion which is hard to shake. The spiritual journey can get caught in the web of playing small when the process of defining self is a way to determine what is safe and what is not safe. The false idea is: if you can find out who you are, you can assert safety and control events.

The illusion of safety may also inspire you to release responsibility for self to another. If you don't trust yourself, then releasing your care to another seems a reasonable choice. However, giving up yourself either leads to more heartache or dysfunction or both. Disempowered, you are disconnected from your center, your source of strength.

In the Akashic Records, the safe road shows up in how you approach your experience. Some will limit the type of questions asked, balking in the face of things too deep or too embarrassing. Others will try opening a couple of times, feel uncomfortable, and never try again. While others stand in the rigidity of I KNOW to create distance, delivering assessments as if they are judging an Olympic event.

You begin within the safety of basics and, over time, build and expand your connection with the Akashic Records. The safe road is not the major portion of your journey.

The deeper road—this is your focus now. To get to this road requires letting go of safe and control and guarantee. The deeper road goes straight into the heart of the unknown, challenging fear, thumbing your nose at blame and doubt, leaving expectation in the dust.

The deeper road doesn't open for you because you're better than, or further along, or higher up. The deeper road opens to you when you lay down your demand to play safe. You willingly move into the unknown because you trust and because truth is the only safety you need now.

Whether you are just beginning your spiritual journey or are further down the path, the deeper road isn't a reward or destination. The deeper road opens because exploring stirs a rare excitement in your soul, makes your heart beat in loving anticipation.

Within the deeper road, you are not worried about whether you are ready because you have accepted yourself as you are in this moment, with love. Your mind is intrigued by your inner light as it prepares you for whatever may be as you enter your deeper road. Gone are the linear blinders, and you freely choose the dynamic perspective of the boundlessness of All That Is.

An end. A beginning. Your life, never to be the same again, because you are no longer limiting yourself to safe ground. You're stepping in for yourself, here, now.

Whatever the deep road is for you—only you can discover! Defining purpose in this moment: learning, loving, soul expressing through this life, a life integrated across the continuum of potential to form, spiritual and physical.

Travel in peace and joy, in love and light.

. . .

Gather what you need, open your Akashic Records, and ask your questions.

1. How do I play safe?
2. What am I afraid of when I don't feel safe?
3. How can I feel safe in the world?
4. How do I hold myself as better than?
5. How can I enter my deep road?

INVITATION

I learned, many years ago, that the journey is never finished because life on the deep road is always about learning in this infinite and eternal moment. In each moment, depth comes through self-acknowledgement of the efforts that brought you to this moment. Self-awareness is not limited. Embraced fully, awareness is available as the infinite and eternal perspective of all of you, body, mind, heart, and soul.

I invite you to give full attention to the powerful effort you have offered yourself in this journey to opening your Akashic Records. Think of all you have learned along the way and how you have changed yourself. Think of the possibility that has come forward and how your life has progressed and expanded — living the same life, with life to never be the same again.

I also invite you to continue this journey, to explore, to step deeper, to learn about the depth and breadth of the Akashic Records. More than either of us can imagine is always available through this connection with the Records. Embrace this abundance as a reflection of your openness and willingness to participate in the fullness of All That Is.

For most, the next step is to learn to open the Akashic Records for Other — which is the next book in this series.

Finally, I invite you to be in touch. I'd love to hear of your journey and to connect. No matter where you are in the world, we are both part of an amazing motion of growth and expansion.

I hope you have found deeper trust within yourself. I also hope you have developed a new relationship with your truth. Trust and truth together will empower you beyond limitation into your heart's deepest desire.

Keep with your practice and learning. Claim the best of your being and becoming. Learn always. Love always. Be yourself always.

Wherever you are in our amazing world, I wish for you the power and wonder of life's journey. May you take pleasure in your adventure into your deep road.

In Joy!

Cheryl

READER BONUS

I have this bonus course for you:
Expand Your Akashic Records Practice
https://www.cherylmarlene.com/akashic-records-masterclass/
Use coupon code: OYAR2021

Akashic Records Starter Kit

**All the tips & discounts you need to begin with
the Akashic Records and
to get to know Cheryl!**

www.cherylmarlene.com/akashic-records-starter-kit/

D on't Forget the Reader's Packet which contains PDFs and an audio recording to support your learning process is also available Download here: https://www.cherylmarlene.com/yourown/

ABOUT CHERYL

www.cherylmarlene.com

Cheryl Marlene, *Akashic Mystic*, is unafraid of the tough, the raw, and the real aspects of doing deep work. She is the world's authority on the Akashic Records and consults in the Akashic Records with clients around the world through Readings, research, and Akashic Future for futuristic business leaders. Students learn to access the Akashic Records through ZENITH her comprehensive and intensive four-level learning program, and her signature classic, *Akashic Records Masterclass*. In the field of consciousness, she is known as a futurist, innovator, and master teacher who delivers life-changing lessons with warmth and humor. Her powerful exploration is cutting edge -- providing you with deep insight today to ignite your vision for tomorrow. Laugh. Learn. Love. Be. Become. Always.

Find Cheryl's Books on her Amazon Author Page or wherever in the world you buy books:

https://www.amazon.com/Cheryl-Marlene/e/B002ZJR8IQ

Cheryl's newest book:

Akashic Records: Gemstone Guardians

https://www.cherylmarlene.com/gemstone-guardians/

Printed in Great Britain
by Amazon

22762482R00145